Contents

AS the Global Sumud Flotilla continues its journey toward Gaza to break the cruel siege that's been starving Palestinian civilians to death, Israeli National Security Minister Itamar Ben-Gvir is pushing to classify all the activists aboard the fleet as terrorists, and to treat them accordingly.

"We will not allow individuals who support terrorism to live in comfort. They will face the full consequences of their actions," Ben-Gvir said. "We must create a clear deterrent. Anyone who chooses to collaborate with Hamas and support terrorism will meet a firm and unyielding response from Israel."

Israel has a very extensive history of raping and torturing prisoners that it has associated with support for designated terrorist groups.

This month's issue is titled "Break The Siege" and features a painting of Greta Thunberg, who is courageously putting everything on the line sailing to Gaza for the second time in fierce opposition to the cruelty of the genocidal regime.

All works are written by Caitlin Johnstone and Tim Foley. The Caitlin Johnstone project is 100 percent reader-funded.

Visit caitlinjohnst.one for the original articles and their supporting links.

It's Not Okay To Be A Grown Adult In August 2025 And Still Believe Lies About Gaza

It's not okay to be a grown adult with internet access in August 2025 and still believe that what we are seeing in Gaza is not a genocide.

It's not okay to be a grown adult with internet access in August 2025 and still believe this mass atrocity is about self-defense.

It's not okay to be a grown adult with internet access in August 2025 and still believe that people in Gaza are not being deliberately starved by Israel.

It's not okay to be a grown adult with internet access in August 2025 and still believe that Israel destroyed Gaza's entire healthcare system because there were Hamas bases in every part of that healthcare system.

It's not okay to be a grown adult with internet access in August 2025 and still believe that Israel is banning foreign journalists from entering Gaza because it is concerned for the journalists' safety.

It's not okay to be a grown adult with internet access in August 2025 and still believe that Israel has been killing a record-shattering number of journalists in Gaza because all of those journalists were Hamas.

It's not okay to be a grown adult with internet access in August 2025 and still believe that Israel has been killing a shocking number of civilians in Gaza because Hamas is using civilians as human shields.

It's not okay to be a grown adult with internet access in August 2025 and still believe that unproven claims made by Israeli officials about what's happening in Gaza should be considered plausible until proven false.

It's not okay to be a grown adult with internet access in August 2025 and still believe that this mass atrocity is about hostages, or is about Hamas, or is about October 7, or is about anything besides the long-sought agenda to remove Palestinians from a Palestinian territory.

It's not okay to be a grown adult with internet access in August 2025 and still believe this is a very complicated issue.

It's not okay to be a grown adult with internet access in August 2025 and still believe that this all started on October 7.

It's not okay to be a grown adult with internet access in August 2025 and still frame an active genocide as a moral gray area with bad actors on both sides.

It's not okay to be a grown adult with internet access in August 2025 and still say you don't know enough about Gaza to have an opinion one way or the other.

It's not okay to be a grown adult with internet access in August 2025 and still support Israel.

It's not okay to be a grown adult with internet access in August 2025 and still support Donald Trump.

It's not okay to be a grown adult with internet access in August 2025 and still support the western power alliance.

It's not okay to be a grown adult with internet access in August 2025 and not be outraged at what you are seeing.

It's not okay to be a grown adult with internet access in August 2025 and not be doing everything you can to end this nightmare.

It's not okay to be a grown adult with internet access in August 2025 and not be doing everything you can to make sure that nothing like this can ever happen again. •

Israel Is Beginning To Choke On Its Own Lies

Netanyahu has confirmed reports that Israel plans an extreme escalation in Gaza which will entail the total military occupation of the entire enclave and the ethnic cleansing of Palestinians, which the Israeli spin machine has termed "voluntary migration".

To be clear, anyone who says the expulsion of Palestinians from Gaza would be "voluntary" is lying. Starving a population and deliberately making their land uninhabitable is exactly the same as forcing them out at gunpoint. Saying "leave or you'll starve" is not meaningfully different from saying "leave or I'll shoot you in the head". Israel's planned mass expulsion will be as forced and involuntary as any in recorded history.

President Trump has fully signed off on this move, washing his hands of the mass atrocity he is cosigning by telling the press that it's going to be "pretty much up to Israel."

Trump is lying. It's up to him. That's why more than 600 former senior Israeli security officials from Mossad and Shin Bet just sent Trump a letter urging him to compel Netanyahu to make peace in Gaza. They understand that the US president has always had the power to end the Gaza holocaust; numerous Israeli insiders have said that this mass atrocity would not be possible without US assistance.

Trump could end all this at any time, and chooses not to. This makes him one of the most evil people in the world.

This whole genocide is powered by lies. Netanyahu just told Fox News that the horrifying aerial footage of the destruction in Gaza that we've been seeing is because every single building in Gaza was booby trapped with explosives by Hamas.

"The reason you see the flattened buildings is because Hamas booby traps every single building," Netanyahu said. "So when we come in, we first have the population moved even though Hamas tries to keep them in the combat zones. But after they move, and we start to move into the neighborhoods that are now populated only by terrorists, they ignite these booby traps. So what we do is we put in an APC, an armored personnel carrier, with a lot of explosives. Detonate it. It sets off all the booby traps and the buildings begin to collapse as a result of that. They're empty buildings, they're not populated buildings."

Absolutely nobody believes this is true. Not one single person alive on this earth sincerely believes that Gaza now looks like a gravel parking lot because Hamas placed explosives inside every single building. Netanyahu doesn't believe it. Israel's most venomous supporters don't believe it. It's just part of the nonstop fountain of lies they are spewing to avoid acknowledging what we all know we're looking at. They've told so many lies by now that they've got to keep lying and lying just to stay afloat, like a man desperately treading water to avoid drowning.

This genocide is one nonstop insult to our intelligence. It's actually degrading at this point. The lies Israel and its supporters have to pretend to believe are getting so ridiculous that supporting Israel is now an act of public humiliation and self-debasement.

Former Israeli prime minister Naftali Bennett has a long rant on his social media accounts complaining that Israel's "status in the United States is collapsing", including among Republicans, with public sentiment turning against them because of what is happening in Gaza.

As you might expect, Bennett does not frame this as a sign that Israel should stop committing genocide in Gaza, but rather complains of a crisis of "antisemitism" in the United States, and accuses Netanyahu of failing to adequately propagandize Americans.

"Jews in the United States are subject to a torrential wave of anti-Semitism, like him I don't remember in my life," Bennett moans, adding, "Antisemites increase to compare the 'hunger' in Gaza to the Holocaust, and thus reduce the memory of the Holocaust. They act that the hunger accusation will haunt israel its citizens, our soldiers, for generations."

"If Netanyahu's propaganda men worked against the enemies of Israel *outside* a tenth of the talent, speed and dedication with which they operate the propaganda machine against their political rivals *inside* israel our situation would be amazing," Bennet writes, saying he wants to "re-establish a rapid and synchronized explanation headquarters".

"Explanation" is the literal translation of the Hebrew word "hasbara", i.e. pro-Israel propaganda.

Meanwhile the term "hasbara" itself is reportedly being abandoned by the Israeli Foreign Ministry, as westerners have come to associate the term with genocide propaganda.

The Times of Israel reports:

> "Long referred to as **hasbara**, a term used to denote both public relations and propaganda that has been freighted with negative baggage in recent years, the ministry now brands its approach as **toda'a** — which translates to 'awareness' or 'consciousness' — an apparent shift toward broader, more proactive messaging."

So they're not abandoning the genocide, and they're not abandoning the genocide propaganda, they're just abandoning the word for the genocide propaganda because people have come to associate that word with propaganda in support of genocide.

The entire Zionist project is built on a foundation of lies. And their lies are starting to catch up with them. They're now at a point where the lies are beginning to damage the public image they're intended to protect.

When a liar is recognized as a liar, his lies will forevermore work only as an antidote to his past lies, and as a light to further expose his intent. From that point on any lie he tells just shows people how ugly his character and intentions really are.

There is no other weapon that works that way. No other weapon which when it's seen immediately stops working, actively disarms the attacker, starts fixing what he broke, and starts attacking him.

Truth will win in the end. •

To Future Generations: They Knew. They All Knew What Was Happening In Gaza.
•Notes From The Edge Of The Narrative Matrix•

A note to future generations for historical record:

Every pundit, politician and reporter of our time who claims they didn't know what was happening in Gaza is lying.

They knew what was happening. They knew Israel was telling lies. They knew about everything.

They had access to the same information as all the rest of us. We watched them make excuses and ignore indisputable facts every step of the way. There was absolutely no confusion about what they were looking at. It was all right out in the open.

Don't let them get away with saying they didn't know. They knew. They knew the entire time. Brand them permanently with this shame, and force them to carry it with them for the rest of their lives.

•

I hate all genocide supporters equally, regardless of their religion. Telling me your religion is like telling me about your dreams: it's completely uninteresting to me. If you support an active genocide you're a bad person who deserves to be shunned and reviled, regardless of what your religion happens to be.

It's so wild how Jewish people will just stride confidently into public discourse about Gaza while strongly emphasizing their Jewishness, as though their support for genocide is somehow special and different from any other asshole's support for genocide. Wanting to starve civilians and mass murder children makes you a piece of shit, whether you are Jewish, Mormon, Buddhist, or atheist.

Nobody cares what religious belief systems you happen to hold in your head while you advocate massacring civilians, they care about the fact that you advocate massacring civilians. Being Jewish doesn't give you some kind of magical immunity from being held to basic moral standards and being judged by society for supporting a mass atrocity. It's got nothing to do with anything.

•

After a whistleblower on the so-called Gaza Humanitarian Foundation named Tony Aguilar shared the heartbreaking story about a boy named Amir who became one of the many Palestinians massacred by Israeli forces while trying to obtain food at an aid site, his family reported that he had been missing since that day and they hadn't known what had happened to him. They still don't know where his body is.

The fact that people just "go missing" in Gaza after being killed indicates Israel often buries the bodies of victims to cover up their deaths — something they've been caught doing before. This is one of many reasons why we can be sure that the actual death toll is much higher than the official record.

•

Still can't believe Israel supporters spent days yelling "Israel isn't starving children, it's starving SICK children!" and thought that was an awesome argument.

•

Friendly periodic reminder that the "Israel bombs hospitals because the hospitals are Hamas bases" narrative was conclusively debunked when IDF soldiers were repeatedly documented entering the hospitals they attacked and destroying individual pieces of medical equipment, one by one. Hamas isn't the target, healthcare is the target. That has been irrefutably established.

•

Opposing the Gaza genocide has meant being proven right about everything from the very beginning every step of the way, hating being proven right, and then having the liberals who kept yelling at you for your rightness slowly begin to acknowledge that you were right, while still finding excuses to hate you for being right anyway.

•

A new poll by the Israel Democracy Institute has found that only 6.7 percent of Jewish Israelis say they are "very troubled" by reports of starvation and suffering in Gaza, with 67 percent saying they are either "not at all troubled" or "not so troubled" by the news. That means those who are pretty much fine with deliberately starving children outnumber those who hold a normal attitude on the matter ten to one.

Poll after poll after poll shows that Jewish Israelis are horrible people who are quantifiably much more cruel and immoral than pretty much any other population. At a certain point you have to stop thinking the polls might be mistaken and see that the only real mistake is Israel.

•

Meanwhile, Ukrainian support for the war with Russia has plunged even further, with a new Gallup poll finding that just 24 percent of Ukrainians now support continuing the fight until victory. A 69 percent supermajority now say they want peace negotiations as soon as possible.

I get called a Putin-loving cryptofascist vatnik tankie Kremlin agent whenever I say this, but a majority of Ukrainians have wanted this war to end for a while now. At this point the only ones who want more war are westerners, plus some of the Ukrainians who live far away from the fighting.

We're being told the holocaust in Gaza can't be ended, and we're being told the war nobody wants in Ukraine must continue. We are ruled by monsters. •

Debating Israel Supporters Is Pointless, Because They Don't Care About Facts Or Morality

If you follow me on Twitter you've probably seen me engaging with Israel supporters to address their arguments, but please don't take this as a suggestion that engaging with Israel supporters is a good idea generally. It isn't.

I engage Zionists online in order to make sure their hasbara damages Israel more than it helps it by using their comments to show everyone that these people always lie about everything, and to familiarize myself with the hasbara talking points of the day so that I can attack them. I do this because I'm a visible figure who writes about this stuff every day for a living, and I've found a very energy-efficient strategy for doing so which doesn't consume too much of my time and focus. For most people there's no good reason to ever engage these freaks at all.

Israel supporters are never, ever engaging in good faith — at least not the ones you're likely to encounter in online spaces. Their goal is never to communicate or to have a conversation, it's to advance the information interests of a genocidal apartheid state. They will say whatever they need to say, and pretend to believe whatever they need to pretend to believe, in order to accomplish this. If you engage them you're not having a normal conversation with a normal person,

you're having a conversation with a psychological operation aimed at manipulating public perception. You're dumping your mental and emotional energy into a black hole, and they are happy to have you waste your energy in that way.

You will never change a Zionist's mind with facts and logic or convince them to reconsider their position using robust argumentation. This is a rare thing to accomplish on any topic because human minds in general tend to bias toward maintaining their preconceived notions, but it's absolutely unheard of when it comes to Israel's supporters. They're not even really listening to you, they're just machine gunning you with whatever words they think will help improve Israel's public image and undermine public trust in its critics.

It is very fruitful to engage and educate people who aren't sure about the genocide in Gaza. It can be fruitful to engage the mainstream liberals who previously defended Biden on Gaza or the Trump voters who are now shaky on the president's Israel First policies. Any normal person with an open mind can be shown the facts and find their way to a truthful and moral understanding of this issue. But you will never move an Israel supporter no matter what you say, because Israel supporters are not interested in facts or morality like normal people are.

If I think of an interesting point to make in response to an Israel supporter online, I'll often just make

8

an article out of it rather than wasting it on them. You can do this too; if you come up with something interesting to say to someone who's defending Israel's atrocities, just turn it into real content for people who are being real. Make a tweet, a blog post, a video, a zine, an email to your local member — something you can aim in a useful direction rather than a completely useless one.

Israelis and their supporters have a much better understanding of the power of manipulating worldwide public perception than the average person. That's why they have a special Hebrew word, hasbara, for this manipulation. Their understanding is so acute that Israel's Foreign Ministry recently changed the name from hasbara to toda'a, because the word hasbara has become too closely associated with genocide propaganda in western minds.

Human consciousness is dominated by mental narrative, so if you can control the narratives which humans are telling about what's going on in the world, you can control the humans. Skillful manipulators understand that power is the ability to control what happens, but true power is the ability to control what people THINK about what happens. That's what we are seeing in all the mass-scale psychological manipulation aimed at making it seem like genocide and ethnic cleansing are totally normal and appropriate things to be happening right now.

Luckily there's only so much manipulation you can use to cover up what people are seeing right in front of their faces. In the short term things look ugly, but in the long term I have a hard time imagining Israel ever recovering from this. All the young people who've witnessed history's first live-streamed genocide are going to be running the world someday, and they are not going to want to have anything to do with the state of Israel.

So anyway, yeah, don't waste your time and energy engaging Zionists. They don't care if anything they're saying is based on truth and morality, and they won't care if anything you say is based on truth and morality. Block them and use your energy on normal people who actually care about telling the truth and doing the right thing, so we can actually bring a stop to this nightmare. •

Israel Assassinates More Journalists To Hide Its Planned War Crimes
•Notes From The Edge Of The Narrative Matrix•

Ahead of a planned Israeli assault on Gaza City which UN officials warn will further exacerbate death and suffering for the Palestinian people, Israel has chosen to assassinate five Al Jazeera journalists who've been stationed there. Among those killed was Anas al-Sharif, one of the most high-profile surviving reporters in Gaza.

The IDF is of course claiming that al-Sharif was Hamas, because that's what they always do. They've been murdering a historically unprecedented number of journalists and defending their systematic effort to blind the world to their actions in Gaza by claiming that every journalist they kill is Hamas. The journalists are Hamas, the hospitals are Hamas, the UN is Hamas, the peace activists are Hamas, the demonstrations are Hamas, telling the truth is Hamas, human empathy is Hamas, objective reality is Hamas. It's all Hamas.

That Israel would feel the need to draw attention to its depravity with this targeted strike at this time shows it has some very ugly intentions for Gaza City that it doesn't want the world to see.

•

One of the many plot holes in Israel's claim that it can't let foreign journalists into Gaza because it's not safe is that there are now huge areas which have been completely captured and controlled by the IDF. That's where the GHF sites are, which is where journalists are most sorely needed right now.

It's not like it's 2023/2024 and journalists would need to follow Israeli forces into Gaza City to document gun battles with Hamas or take their crews through areas where the IDF could be carrying out air strikes. They could safely just set up their cameras at aid distribution sites and document what's happening.

The only reason this hasn't occurred is because Israel doesn't want the world to see what it's doing at those aid distribution sites. There is absolutely no other explanation.

•

British police arrested 522 people for holding signs saying "I oppose genocide, I support Palestine Action" in response to their government banning the activist group as a terrorist organization. Nearly half of those arrested were over sixty years old.

When I was young and naive I thought terrorism looks like someone detonating a car bomb or crashing planes into skyscrapers. Now that I'm mature and educated I know that terrorism actually looks like an elderly woman holding a sign saying people should be allowed to oppose genocide.

This is a society that has gone stark raving insane.

•

U2 frontman Bono has finally issued a statement calling for peace in Gaza two years into a genocide, and however bad you expected it to be I guarantee it's worse.

He works his way through pretty much every pro-genocide Israeli talking point while pretending to care about Palestinians. He spends paragraphs on October 7, mentions the word "Hamas" 14 times, falsely claims "Hamas are using starvation as a weapon in the war," says "Hamas had deliberately positioned themselves under civilian targets, having tunneled their way from

school to mosque to hospital," babbles about the 1988 Hamas charter while ignoring its 2017 revisions, blames the whole thing on Netanyahu, and of course mentions "Israel's right to exist."

I seriously think he hit every major hasbara talking point. I don't think he missed a single one. It's genocide propaganda disguised as humanitarianism. Bono is a piece of shit.

•

I judge the character of Jewish people based on how much they oppose the genocide in Gaza. This is also how I judge the character of anyone who is not Jewish.

•

As soon as someone says they support Israel for religious reasons, you can dismiss anything they say in defense of Israel's actions, because you know they'll tell any lie and promote any kind of propaganda in order to advance their religious mission. They're not engaging the subject to share facts and communicate, they're engaging it to obtain promised rewards in the afterlife and please an invisible deity. They'll say whatever they need to say in order to make this happen.

Think about it. If you sincerely held the religious belief that Israel needs to be supported no matter what in order to fulfill some kind of prophecy, or that if you don't promote the interests of Israel you'll be tortured for eternity in Hell, or that Actual Metaphysical Yahweh has commanded that helping Israel is the single most important thing in the world, would you not say whatever you need to say and promote whatever narratives you need to promote in order to help make that happen? Of course you would. It's not about facts and truth for such people, it's about getting into Heaven and bringing back Jesus and stuff.

The instant someone admits to supporting Israel for religious reasons, there's no reason to believe anything else they say. Because you know they'll say things they don't really know to be true and pretend to believe things they don't really believe in order to do what they've been told is the most important thing they can possibly do with their lives. It's impossible to have a truth-based conversation with such a person. •

Stopping The Gaza Holocaust Is The First Step Toward A Healthy World

Nicole on Facebook writes, "I would love to hear you explain how Palestine is the moral question of our time. Why it's so important. How it's related to every movement and should be a concern to everyone."

Palestine is the moral question of our time because the abuse of the Palestinians is the most glaring, in-your-face symptom of the imperial disease. You can see the effects of so many of the empire's abusive dynamics in how this thing is playing out, from racism to colonialism to militarism to war profiteering to mass media propaganda to empire-building to government corruption to suppression of free speech to ecocide to the heartless, mindless, soul-eating nature of the capitalist system under which we all live.

But there's more to it than that. The primary reason to place Palestine front and center as the moral issue of our time is because if we can't sort out the morality of an active genocide backed by our own western governments, we're not going to be able to sort out anything else. Stopping the Gaza holocaust and bringing justice to the Palestinians is the very first step toward a healthy civilization.

Palestine is the moral issue of our time for the same reason if you saw someone in your family torturing another member of your family to death, it would be the most urgent matter happening in your life at that moment. You'd have other problems in your life, but that would come first.

If we're the sort of society that would allow a live-streamed genocide to take place with the support of our own government and its allies, then we're not the sort of society that can steer away from its trajectory toward dystopia and armageddon. If you're the sort of individual who would allow a live-streamed genocide to take place with the support of your own government and its allies, then you're not the sort of individual who can help steer our species away from disaster.

Gaza is not the only thing that matters in the world. But if you're not forcefully opposing the Gaza holocaust, you definitely don't have a healthy enough conscience to address any of the world's other problems.

I sometimes see Israel supporters refer to pro-Palestine sentiment as "virtue signaling", which is funny because it means they view themselves as holding the unpopular, unvirtuous position. But really there's nothing particularly virtuous about supporting Gaza, and it's not some cool, special thing you'd want to signal about yourself. It's just what you do when you're not an extremely shitty person. It's the basic, bare-minimum expectation of normal human morality.

I don't want to be friends with anyone who doesn't oppose the Gaza holocaust. I don't want to follow any commentators or analysts who don't speak out against the Gaza holocaust. At this point I don't even want to listen to any music or read any poetry from people who don't take a stand against the Gaza holocaust. Since 2023 I've moved from rejecting anyone who actively sided with Israel to rejecting anyone who is even complicit in their silence.

The other day I saw some Australian influencer forcefully trying to assert that it's okay not to take a position on Gaza, and nobody in her replies was buying it. Supporting Israel and aligning with US foreign policy comes with a lot of career benefits for high-profile individuals, and you don't get to both enjoy those perks and also keep ethical people interested in what you have to say. You can't have it both ways. You have to choose between the perks and the people. You actually do.

Opposition to the Gaza holocaust is the very first step in assessing if someone is worth my time. If you can't even meet the basic, bare-minimum expectation of opposing an active genocide, then you are too callous and apathetic to be my friend. If you can't even get this basic, kindergarten-level moral question right, then your mind is too shallow and your heart too hardened for me to be interested in your analysis, your ideas, your politics, or your art.

There are so many terrible things in our world, and there is so much work that needs to be done to address them. I don't know what ideas, strategies and movements will get us out of this mess, but I do know that if any are going to emerge they're going to come from the people who've been taking a strong stand against Israel and its western allies these last two years. Those are the individuals, movements, and political factions to pay attention to going forward. Nobody else is equipped to help. •

The Two-State Solution Sham, And Other Reader Questions

I'm just going to answer questions from readers for a while.

•

Lorna asks on Facebook, "Is the 2 state solution a solution ...or a delusion??"

Israeli officials have been telling us themselves that it's a delusion for a while now, and I think we should believe them. Everything about Israel is stacked against allowing the creation of a Palestinian state, and even if the Palestinians do get a meaningful state somehow, what then? Israel is constantly at war with its neighbors who refuse to obey its dictates, so a "Palestinian state" would likely either be (A) Israel continuing to bomb and massacre Palestinians just like they're doing now, or (B) Palestinians obeying the dictates of Tel Aviv and not being meaningfully sovereign.

The truth is that Palestinians will never be free as long as Israel exists as the hypermilitaristic racist settler-colonialist state that it is. The way to have peace and freedom is to give everyone equal rights, grant right of return for displaced Palestinians, right the wrongs of the past, and for Israel and its western allies to pay so many reparations to Palestinians that the wounds of the past are no longer felt by future generations.

Israelis will never go along with this unless they are forced to, but they won't stop any of their evils unless they are forced to anyway. The world is going to have to force them to stop, just like it had to force Nazi Germany to stop.

•

Christine asks on Substack, "What do you do for self care? You spend so much time fighting the good cause, does Mr F look after you well?"

Mr F (my husband Tim Foley for those who don't know) gives me a full-body massage for one hour every day. We go through so many massage oils I've been ordering big professional-sized jugs from an industrial supplier. I also take baths when I'm feeling overwhelmed.

Mostly though the key for both of us is tons of inner work. We've got an energetic practice we developed on our own for healing trauma and getting rid of inner fixations, and when we're feeling overwhelmed we can just discharge the energy. Tim places more emphasis on nonduality and eastern spirituality in his practice, while my practices are more somatic in nature. Over the years we've gotten very good at talking each other through whatever issues we're going through at any point in time.

I don't understand how anyone engages with this stuff without tons of inner work. I know I personally would have drowned in the darkness of the world a long time ago if I wasn't healing my way through this thing.

•

Naterian asks on Twitter, "When did you first become aware of the injustice in palestine? What year, what age were you, what event was it that fully opened your eyes to how dire the situation was?"

My father taught me about the plight of the Palestinians back in the early eighties, which he had initially learned about from some people distributing literature in the city mall. After that it was a few different experiences over the years that opened my eyes wider bit by bit, including my troubling encounters with Israeli tourists while traveling in South America and watching Israeli snipers fire on unarmed protesters in 2018.

And actually my eyes are still being opened. Israel still finds ways to shock me with its abusiveness and depravity to this very day. Just when I think I've seen the full scope of its evil, I find more. I'm learning more about the kind of malice and tyranny that Palestinians have been living under every day.

•

Tom asks on Substack, "What's going to happen after recognition?"

It's not clear at this time that much of anything will happen after governments like the UK, France, Canada and Australia go through with their planned recognition of a Palestinian state. What are they going to do, plant a Palestinian flag in the rubble of Gaza? Hand people Palestinian passports while they're being rounded up in concentration camps in preparation for mass deportations?

The immediate problem right now isn't that Palestinians don't have a state, it's that Israel has spent the last two years capitalizing on the rare window of political will which was afforded by October 7 to rapidly push through as many of its pre-existing military agendas as it possibly can. That's not going to be stopped by giving a diplomatic thumbs-up to Palestinian statehood, it's going to be stopped by imposing costs which outweigh the benefits of what Israel is doing.

Hard economic sanctions. The termination of military and arms agreements. Making Israel a pariah state in every possible way. Collectively threatening to terminate alliances with the United States in order to pressure the US to bring Israel to heel.

Israelis have an acute understanding of the difference between narrative and real material benefits. They're happy to keep doing what they like and grabbing as many hard material benefits as they can while western governments make performative gestures that amount to nothing but narrative. They'll let us have our narratives as long as they get the material land grabs and strategic gains they're after. It's not until the material costs outweigh the material benefits that they'll stop acting the way they are acting.

•

Barbarism Critic writes on Twitter, "As a budding writer who loves your work I would love to hear your best advice for how to stay fresh and write consistently when you start to feel like your retreading the same waters again and again."

I think being really obsessive helps, to be honest. Making a vocation out of this thing instead of just something you do here and there means you're always pointing at it and coming up with different angles and fresh ideas, even when the news cycle hasn't changed much.

The daily news is an endless source of new material. Right now Antiwar. com and Drop Site News are the best resources for finding important news updates on what the empire is up to from day to day, and Antiwar's Dave DeCamp has a great show on YouTube which he puts out every weekday breaking down the latest moves of the imperial war machine. You can pick any story that sparks your interest and just write whatever you reckon about it.

And again I have to point toward inner work as an essential component of this. Writing can't flow freely from expansive directions if you're in a state of inner turmoil all the time, and as you explore your psyche you'll have all kinds of new insights which tie into what's going on in the world in all kinds of ways.

Also please remember that there are two of me; everything you read here comes from both me and Tim, so

15

you shouldn't see it as a problem if your volume isn't the same as ours. Being a team of two means we've got twice as much time and energy for both writing and research, and if one of us gets busy or has an off day the other can pick up the slack. We're also constantly in conversation about this stuff inspiring each other and coming up with new ideas. I've seen individual writers beat themselves up about not being able to write new stuff every day like Caitlin Johnstone does, as though "Caitlin Johnstone" is just one person and not a team of two.

•

Sinwa asks on Facebook, "Where do you think it will all end?"

Honestly? I reckon we win this thing. In the short term things look ugly, but in the big picture people are waking up to the reality of the empire at a rate that would have been unthinkable a few years ago. As a species we're getting better and better at networking and sharing information with each other, while the empire is getting more ham-fisted and obvious every day. I can't see that trajectory continuing in a way that works out well for our rulers.

It's taboo to express optimism on the internet, but I'm honestly more optimistic about beating these bastards than I've ever been before. It's scary and nasty now, but the scariest and nastiest moments in my abusive first marriage happened right before I got out. If I told you I'm pessimistic about our future, I'd be lying. I think we win, and I think we get a healthy world. •

Gaza Doesn't Need Our Tears, It Needs Our Anger

Celebrities are finally speaking out about Gaza after two years of genocide, but there's been something off about it that hasn't been sitting right. A Palestinian named Maria Odeh Fakhouri made a great point on Instagram which put her finger on it:

Notice how celebrities speaking up now aren't really all that angry. Their statements are about "heartbreak" and sadness.

They are modeling passivity to the masses as we enter into this next stage of societal awareness.

They communicate to their fans: be sad about genocide but ignore it for awhile first. And then start talking about how sad it is a couple of years later.

They are agents of colonial brainwashing.

I feel this so hard. Gaza doesn't need our sadness, it needs out anger. It needs our rage. That's the only appropriate response to a live-streamed genocide supported by your own government.

Sadness and grief are for natural disasters. Cancer diagnoses. Terrible accidents. This is not something that has passively happened to the people of Gaza, it's something that's been done to them by other people,

and the people who are doing it have names and faces. It's not a tragedy, it's a crime. A crime that is still currently being perpetrated and urgently needs to be stopped, by any means necessary.

The correct response is rage. Rage toward the people who are responsible for this mass atrocity. The officials of the Israeli government and all their western allies. Their apologists and propagandists in the mainstream press. The war profiteers who are benefiting from an active genocide. Individual members of the IDF. The hasbarists who swarm social media and pollute our information ecosystem with manipulation and lies.

Celebrities and influencers who urge us to weep for Gaza are pushing us into passivity and defeatism by urging us to treat this like an unavoidable tragedy that has already happened instead of an unforgivable atrocity that is still underway. This is power-serving propaganda, and it deserves nothing but scorn.

People often use anger in unwholesome ways in our society, but that doesn't mean there's not a healthy place for it. Every human emotion has healthy applications and unhealthy applications, and anger is no different. When someone is crossing a line which does harm to someone else, anger is an entirely appropriate and correct response in that moment, and when it's applied consciously and with care it can yield very positive results. Sometimes

people need to be pushed back to the other side of the line they are crossing with red hot heat.

Emotions are tools; they only become unhealthy when those tools are pointed at things other than their intended purpose. Anger at someone who made an innocent mistake. Delight in the suffering of others. Sadness and heartbreak in the face of monstrous injustice. These are emotions applied incorrectly.

Do not weep for Gaza. Rage for Gaza. Protest for Gaza. Take direct action for Gaza. Ruin people's day for Gaza. Ruin people's careers for Gaza. Don't let the facilitators of this nightmare have a moment's peace. Don't let them go on with their lives like what they did was no big deal. This isn't sad, it's enraging. And it deserves a response of unmitigated forceful aggression. •

The Biblical Case For Supporting Israel

During a speech in South Carolina, US Senator Lindsey Graham warned that God will "pull the plug" on Americans if they stop supporting Israel.

"This is not a hard choice if you're an American. It's not a hard choice if you're a Christian," Graham said. "A word of warning: if America pulls the plug on Israel, God will pull the plug on us. And we're not going to let that happen."

The senator is correct, of course.

What, do you doubt him? God clearly and explicitly commands Christians to support the modern state of Israel. It's right here in the Holy Bible; give me a moment and I'll find the verse for you.

Aha! Got it. Exodus 20:13, "You shall not murder."

Wait, hold on, that's not it.

Here it is, Matthew 5:9, "Blessed are the peacemakers."

Hang on, shoot, that's not the one. What I meant to say is Lamentations 2:19, "Lift your hands to him for the lives of your children, who faint for hunger at the head of every street."

Ah, wrong one, lemme thumb through this a bit more. Got it! Proverbs 24:11, "Rescue those who are being taken away to death; hold back those who are stumbling to the slaughter."

Wait, sorry, no, it's Psalm 101:7, "No one who practices deceit shall dwell in my house; no one who utters lies shall continue before my eyes."

Oh no actually it's Proverbs 6:16-19, "There are six things that the Lord hates, seven that are an abomination to him: haughty eyes, a lying tongue, and hands that shed innocent blood, a heart that devises wicked plans, feet that make haste to run to evil, a false witness who breathes out lies, and one who sows discord among brothers."

Oops, no, it's definitely not that one. Actually it's Deuteronomy 27:25, "Cursed be anyone who takes a bribe to shed innocent blood."

No, dang it, that makes AIPAC recipients sound bad. Gimme a minute. Ah! Mark 12:31, "You shall love your neighbor as yourself."

No, wait, got it! Here it is, Romans 14:19, "Let us therefore make every effort to do what leads to peace and to mutual edification."

Oh no, that isn't the one I was looking for, it was Second Corinthians 13:11, "Strive for full restoration, encourage one another, be of one mind, live in peace. And the God of love and peace will be with you."

Oh actually that one sounds kind of antisemitic in this context, gimme a sec.

Got it! Ephesians 4:3, "Make every effort to keep the unity of the Spirit through the bond of peace."

Hold on, that's not it either. The one I meant to cite was Hebrews 12:14, "Make every effort to live in peace with everyone and to be holy; without holiness no one will see the Lord."

Oh boy, this really isn't going well. Lemme see… oh! James 3:18, "Peacemakers who sow in peace reap a harvest of righteousness."

Gosh darn it, I made a mistake. The verse I meant to point to was First Peter 3:11, "They must turn from evil and do good; they must seek peace and pursue it."

Wait, no, it was Galatians 5:22, "But the fruit of the Spirit is love, joy, peace, forbearance, kindness, goodness, faithfulness, gentleness and self-control."

Actually it was Luke 6:35–36, "But love your enemies, do good to them, and lend to them without expecting to get anything back. Then your reward will be great, and you will be children of the Most High, because he is kind to the ungrateful and wicked. Be merciful, just as your Father is merciful."

Oops, no, nope. Man this is way harder than I thought it was going to be. Oh! Hey! Found it! It was right here in Genesis the whole time, chapter 12, verse 3: "I will bless those who bless you, and whoever curses you I will curse; and all peoples on earth will be blessed through you."

There! See? It's right there in black and white. God's saying we are commanded to support a modern state that we created in 1948, no matter what it does. The Bible is entirely clear and unequivocal about this, and says absolutely nothing to the contrary.

Checkmate, heathen. •

Stop Giving Israeli Officials A Media Platform To Spout Lies

Australia's state broadcaster the ABC gave extensive airtime to Israeli deputy foreign affairs minister Sharren Haskel on Friday, allowing her to voice her objections to Australian demonstrations against the very genocide that she and her government are presently committing in Gaza.

Haskel's statements were then picked up and printed in outlets like The Guardian, quoting at length her lies denying Israel's deliberate starvation of Palestinians and her assertion that anti-genocide protesters are "useful idiots" who fell for "terrorist propaganda".

In an effort to give equal weight to both sides of the issue, The Guardian also quotes a response from a spokesperson for the Palestine Action Group, which helped coordinate the massive march over the Sydney Harbour Bridge earlier this month.

"The only useful idiots here are those in the media who continue to print Israeli propaganda despite two years of being consistently lied to," the spokesperson said.

I don't know how anyone could possibly disagree with this. It's absolutely ridiculous to be giving these freaks a platform to spout lies in the latter half of the year 2025.

Stop platforming Israeli government officials and professional genocide apologists. Stop asking them what they think. Stop presenting their lies and manipulations as news stories. Stop asking them if they agree with their critics. Stop doing it. Stop.

Who cares if the government official who is perpetrating a genocide is offended by people saying she's committing genocide? Who cares if a murderer dislikes being called a murderer while in the middle of an act of murder? Who cares if it hurts their feelings to be told they're doing the thing that they are doing? Who gives a single solitary fuck?

Of course the people **committing the genocide** don't want people saying they're committing genocide. Of course they don't. It does not matter. It's completely irrelevant. Stop treating that like it's a news story.

Every major human rights group on earth says this is a genocide, including Israeli groups. Genocide scholars and human rights experts around the world are in overwhelming in agreement on this. Once a consensus has been reached on that scale, there is no longer any journalistic obligation to keep asking **the people doing the genocide** whether they agree that it's a genocide or how it makes their feelings feel to hear people say that it is.

The facts at this point are so well-established that continuing to give them a broad platform and report on what they say is the same as platforming people who believe Hitler was a good guy who should have finished the job. The only moral difference is that Hitler's genocide is over so news outlets wouldn't be actively helping him perpetrate an active genocide like they are in the case of Israel.

We need to make Israel and its supporters own the shame of their lies. When you've got Netanyahu telling Fox News that Gaza looks the way it looks because Hamas put explosives inside "every single building", that's the kind of lie that's meant to humiliate you. It's commanding a slave to believe two plus two equals five just to demonstrate how completely dominated they are.

It's a public humiliation ritual, and **they** should be the ones who are humiliated. In a normal situation, someone saying that Gaza looks like a gravel parking lot because Hamas put explosives in all the buildings would be looked at like they were wearing a gimp mask while covered in bodily fluids in public.

It's just so submissive and cucky. The hospitals are all Hamas bases. UNRWA is a Hamas stronghold. The journalists are all terrorists. The starving civilians aren't really starving. Civilians are dying in such high numbers because there are Hamas members hiding behind all the civilians. The UN, Human Rights Watch, Amnesty International and all major human rights groups all say the things they say because they

secretly hate Jews. This obvious land grab is actually about hostages and October 7. Stating self-evident facts is antisemitic blood libel.

These aren't just lies, they are insults to our intelligence. They are intended to degrade and humiliate us. To believe them is an exercise in self-debasement. They may as well be literally urinating on us and demanding that we say it's raining.

This is backwards. We're not the ones who should feel humiliated. We're not the ones presenting these ridiculous fairytales as true. We're not the ones committing genocide. This is their shame. It belongs to them. And we will know we've won when this is how their lies and atrocities get treated in mainstream discourse. The shame will be placed directly where it belongs.

We will know things have moved toward health when the standard response to an Israel apologist telling obvious lies is a knee-jerk "How embarrassing for you to have to say that like you think it's true. You're either a liar or a sucker, and either way, shame on you. You're either a deceitful freak trying to psychologically manipulate me into supporting the worst things in the world, or you're a moronic dupe who's debased themselves by swallowing obvious lies. Either way it's a pathetic, disgusting, shameful way to live."

When we've moved toward health this will be the standard response, whether it's in day to day

conversation, online interactions, or someone spouting lies on a mainstream punditry show. This is the healthy response to atrociously shameful behavior. •

Israel Is So Evil That It Has A Military Unit Dedicated To Excusing Atrocities
•Notes From The Edge Of The Narrative Matrix•

Israel is so fucking evil that it has a military unit dedicated to coming up with excuses for the IDF's atrocities. +972 reports that the IDF has a special unit it calls the "Legitimization Cell", because it is tasked with finding justifications to legitimize the assassination of journalists and other war crimes for the purpose of "public relations".

Probably goes without saying, but if Israel was on the side of truth and morality it would not have a military unit dedicated to manipulating the public narrative about actions which normal people would see as extremely evil.

•

Israel: We can't allow Palestinian journalists to remain alive in Gaza because all the Palestinian journalists are Hamas.

Western journalists: Okay so let us in, that way there can be journalists documenting what's happening in Gaza who aren't Hamas.

Israel: [long pause] ... No.

•

I have never been less open to people with different opinions than I am with Gaza. I am simply correct, and if you disagree with me you are wrong and I hate you.

I have alienated various readers and online factions over the years with the things I have written, but that has usually been unintentional; normally I don't like to alienate people who resonate with my work. Gaza was the first time I've been happy to lose anyone who disagreed with me. It was like, You're leaving? Good. Get the fuck out. I'm going to keep saying what I'm saying and if you don't like it then I don't like you. If you don't leave then I'll kick you out myself.

I like to stay open to different perspectives, and I like to have people with different perspectives stay open to me. But Gaza is such an easy and obvious moral question that I stand nothing to gain from any contact with anybody who answers that question incorrectly. I've never been so fast and so confident in making enemies than I have over this issue.

I'm nearly as impatient with people who haven't taken a forceful side on this. It's a sign of developing maturity to be able to see both sides of an issue, but it's a sign of further maturity to understand that just because you can see both sides doesn't mean you shouldn't take sides on important and relevant moral issues with a clear right and wrong side. Stop fence-sitting on a genocide and grow the fuck up.

If a guy tries to rob you or rape you or murder you make sure you ask him his religion before trying to stop him, because you don't want to be accidentally antisemitic.

•

Nothing creates support for Hamas more than Israel's actions in Gaza. Nothing creates hatred of Israel more than Israel's actions in Gaza. Nothing creates hatred of Jews more than Israel's actions in Gaza. Everything Israel's supporters complain most about is caused by Israel.

•

The strongest argument that Israel is committing genocide is that all major human rights groups say it's a genocide, including Human Rights Watch, Amnesty International, and Israeli rights groups like B'Tselem, along with the overwhelming majority of genocide scholars and human rights experts. The debate is over. This is a settled matter.

The hasbara machine hasn't come up with a counter-argument for this. They hate it. Whenever I use it they always try to push the debate in some other direction where they have a counter-argument they've been trained to regurgitate, but when I stick to the universal consensus among human rights groups they always get mad and rage quit.

•

It's so undignified how western governments and news outlets keep talking about Israel's officially stated reasons for its actions in Gaza like we don't all know they want to get rid of the Palestinians who live there and have been trying to get rid of them for generations.

•

I love when I criticize Israel for something and someone goes "Oh yeah well America does that too!" Like that's a defense. It's like yes, those are both evil states who do evil things constantly, and they work in conjunction with each other and are not meaningfully separate. Yes.

•

Being an ally of Israel or the United States is immoral for many reasons, but this is especially the case during their joint genocide project in Gaza. They should both be made pariah states.

•

Start recognizing Palestinian humanity and then maybe I'll take you seriously when you talk about recognizing a Palestinian state.

•

Opposition to the Gaza holocaust has always been led from the bottom up. It started with Palestinians documenting their own genocide, then ordinary westerners saw this and began opposing it, then slowly the media and mainstream human rights organizations began following the leadership of the people and applying scrutiny to Israel's atrocities, and then, even more slowly, western governments began feebly pushing back on Israel.

This has all happened in response to widespread public outcry forcing the western political/media class to respond. The mass media cannot retain its legitimacy in the eyes of the public if it keeps churning out brazen genocide propaganda without ever scrutinizing Israel. Governments cannot retain the consent of the governed if they completely ignore a mass atrocity that the public cares deeply about. So they were forced to start moving, or else risk the public turning on them.

The primary lesson here is that we must keep pushing this issue as hard as we can, because it's working. They can't ignore us anymore, and they're feeling the pressure. Their response has been painfully weak and inadequate, but it's infinitely more than we were seeing in the early months of the genocide. We need to keep hammering this thing.

The second lesson here is that our "leaders" are not actually our leaders. We are leading them on the most important moral issue of our time, and they are following us. It is an absolute certainty that western governments and media would be ignoring Gaza if the public had ignored it too. They definitely wanted us to ignore it, and for a long time it really seemed like they expected us to get exhausted and drop it. It wasn't until we made it clear that this isn't getting shuffled down the memory hole with the daily news churn that we really began to see things change.

We are leading this dance. So we need to keep leading. Keep driving. Keep pushing. The louder our voices get, the more movement we see from them.

So don't stop. •

Some Suggestions

Pay attention to the mainstream media, but only so you're aware what the bastards want you to think. The western press are plutocrat-controlled propaganda services for the US-centralized capitalist empire, and they frame their output accordingly. Don't trust them.

Be aware of online echo chambers and confirmation bias, and be humble enough to understand that these things affect you. Make sure you're getting information from a variety of sources, including ones you disagree with ideologically. It's easy to spin off into erroneous perspectives if you don't have any other feedback keeping you in check.

Ignore our society's ideas about what an ideal or successful life looks like. This is a sick civilization whose madness is driving us all into dystopia and disaster. Blaze your own path, and set your own standards for what a good and worthy life would look like.

Make a practice of noticing beauty everywhere. Everything has beauty, even the ugliest things you can imagine. If you can't see the beauty in what you are perceiving in a given moment, the failure is in the eye of the beholder. Beauty is just the experience of having truly seen something.

Feel your feelings fully and courageously, all the way through. If you have forgotten how to cry, re-learn. Don't repress your feelings, but don't make them anyone else's problem either. Feelings are meant to be felt. That's all.

Face your inner demons and heal them. Don't hurt anyone else with them. If you have children, make this a priority of the most urgent order, because you will pass your woundedness onto them if you don't. You can't heal all that's wrong in the world, but you can heal all that's wrong in you.

Put love before everything in life. No one ever went to their grave wishing they had loved less, or had placed their career or ambition above their children or their partner. Love with everything in you; hold nothing back. Loss is inevitable in a mortal life, but love anyway, because it's the only thing that makes a mortal incarnation worth it in the first place.

Learn to love yourself. This looks like bringing a passionate, unconditional "YES" to everything that shows up inside you — all your thoughts, feelings, sensations etc, even the ones you don't like very much right now. If you feel resistance to this, bring a "YES" to that resistance. Keep YESing all the resistances until you work your way in. You can only love others to the extent that you love yourself.

Hold no loyalties to the collective delusions of your family, your social circle, or your culture. If you know they're wrong or ridiculous about something, there's no reason to protect it or act like it's legitimate. Be free from the psychological shackles of conformism. Life is too short for that shit.

Open yourself up to new music, films and art, and increase your capacity for appreciating and enjoying culture outside your comfort zone. Learning how to appreciate more things will make life more enjoyable for you.

Be discerning about what you put into your body. A system of food production and distribution which is guided entirely by the pursuit of profit will not have your health interests at heart in the options it presents you with.

Be kind to people who struggle with neuroses, but try your best to free yourself from your own. Certain segments of our society have become far too glorifying of psychological dysfunction and far too encouraging of learned helplessness and irresponsibility. Be a mature adult and heal everything you are capable of healing, and for everything else try to find adaptations and strategies to get by.

Cultivate a serene mind. If you feel called to, pursue spiritual enlightenment. It's entirely achievable and readily available.

Do as much as you can to make the world a better place, and be content with your efforts regardless of whether or not they are successful. You'll never be able to save the world single-handedly no matter what you can do; all you can do is make one person's worth of effort. Make peace with that. •

Israelis Understand That Trump Can End The Nightmare In Gaza. Americans Should Know This Too.

It's so revealing how Israelis keep begging Trump to end the killing in Gaza, because they understand that the US president has the power to force Israel to stop. It seems like Israelis understand this far better than Americans do.

Six former Israeli hostages and the widow of a slain hostage have released a video pleading with President Trump in English to support a comprehensive deal to make peace in Gaza so that the remaining hostages can be freed.

"You have the power to make history, to be the president of peace, the one who ended the war, ended the suffering, and brought every hostage home, including my little brother," implores one of the hostages.

"President Trump, please act now before it's too late for them, too," pleads the widow.

This is not the first time Israelis have begged Trump to force an end to the slaughter. Earlier this month more than 600 former senior Israeli security officials from Mossad and Shin Bet sent Trump a letter urging him to compel Netanyahu to make peace in Gaza. They did this because they understand something that many Americans do not: that the US president has always had the power to end the Gaza holocaust.

It's crazy how many times I've encountered Americans telling me that this is "Israel's war" and there's nothing the president can do to end it. It was mostly Democrats doing this back when Biden was president and I was slamming Genocide Joe for continuing this mass atrocity, and now that Trump is in office it's his supporters who show up in my comments section white knighting for the president.

"It's not our war and we should stay out of it," they sometimes claim, mistakenly thinking that critics of the US-backed genocide are asking for some kind of US intervention.

But the call isn't for the US to intervene, it's for the US to stop intervening. To end the US interventionism that has been underway for two years. The Gaza holocaust can be ended by the US simply ceasing to add wood to the fire.

Israeli military insiders have been saying again and again that the onslaught in Gaza would not be possible without US support.

A senior Israeli air force official told Haaretz last year that "without the Americans' supply of weapons to the Israel Defense Forces, especially the air force, Israel would have had a hard time sustaining its war for more than a few months."

In November 2023 retired Israeli Major General Yitzhak Brick told Jewish News Syndicate that, "All of our missiles, the ammunition, the precision-guided bombs, all the airplanes and bombs, it's all from the US. The minute they turn off the tap, you can't keep fighting. You have no capability. … Everyone understands that we can't fight this war without the United States. Period."

Former Israeli prime minister Ehud Olmert wrote the following last year:

> "The entire Israel Air Force relies completely on American aircraft: fighter planes, transport planes, refueler planes and helicopters. All of Israel's air power is based on the American commitment to defend Israel. We have no other reliable source for essential supplies of equipment, munitions and advanced weapons that Israel cannot manufacture on its own. In recent months, hundreds of American transport planes have landed at IAF bases carrying thousands of tons of advanced, vital military equipment and munitions."

The Israelis clearly understand that they've been entirely dependent on the US for the IDF's acts of butchery in Gaza this entire time, and they clearly understand that the US president has the ability to turn off the tap whenever he wants.

And now they are begging the president to do so with increasing urgency, because it's been made clear to them that their own government isn't going to stop until it is forced to stop. They can't stop the gunman, so they're turning to the man who's feeding him the ammo.

It would be good if Americans understood this as well. Trump is committing genocide in Gaza, just as surely as Netanyahu is, and he could end it at any time. The fact that he still has not chosen to do so makes him one of the most evil people on earth. •

The US Treats Israeli Pedophiles Nicer Than Wounded Palestinian Kids
•Notes From The Edge Of The Narrative Matrix•

Antiwar has a story out right now with the headline "Rep. Greene: US Should Let Gaza Children in for Medical Treatment, Prosecute Israeli Child Predators."

It's a headline that says so much about what's going on in the world in just a few words. Is the US really not letting Gaza children in for medical treatment? Is the US really failing to prosecute Israelis who prey on children? Why are these necessary things to say? And why is it being left to Marjorie Taylor Greene to say them?

What's crazy is that these are entirely true and legitimate grievances, as Antiwar's Dave DeCamp explains:

> "The Georgia representative was referring to a recent State Department decision to block visas for Palestinians from Gaza in response to outrage from pro-Trump activist Laura Loomer over wounded Palestinian children arriving for medical treatment, and the case of Tom Alexandrovich, a senior Israeli cybersecurity official who was arrested in a sting operation in Nevada for attempting to lure a child for sexual purposes but was allowed to go back to Israel."

I mean, damn.

Things are so fucked up that the only way to get wounded Palestinian children in and out of the United States for medical treatment these days would be to disguise them as Israeli pedophiles.

•

Israel apologists are still trying to make "we're not starving children, we're starving SICK children" work. Bari Weiss's media outlet The Free Press has a new genocide apologia article out noting that twelve of the emaciated children we've seen in photos distributed by the mainstream press have had preexisting conditions like "cystic fibrosis, rickets, or other serious ailments."

This argument is exactly the same as starting a fire in a crowded building and then claiming you can't be guilty of murder by arson because many of the people who died in the fire were handicapped and elderly individuals who couldn't escape quickly enough. Everyone knows the people who suffer first and worst in a famine are small children, the elderly, and the sick.

As others have pointed out, it really shows how desperate the Israel spinmeisters are getting that they would cite "rickets" as a pre-existing condition in their argument to dismiss concerns about starvation in Gaza, given that rickets is a condition caused by malnutrition.

•

Israel: We have to kill all the journalists in Gaza because they're Hamas.

Western journalists: Okay so let us in so at least someone's there to report what's happening in Gaza.

Israel: We can't, it's not safe for you.

Western journalists: Why not?

Israel: Because then YOU'D be Hamas.

•

Saw a tweet from former Israeli prime minister Naftali Bennett complaining that "Europe is becoming Islamized," fearmongering about the number of Muslims who now live in some of Europe's major cities.

Israelis are something else, man. They don't want Muslims to live in the middle east, they don't want Muslims to live in Europe. Kinda seems like they just don't want Muslims to live.

•

The New York Post has an article out with the headline "Queens bodega named 'Gaza Deli and Grill' ignites fear among Jewish New Yorkers — including Oct. 7 survivor: 'I'm still not safe'".

It's just as ridiculous as it sounds. There's a bodega in New York called "Gaza Deli and Grill" and Jewish locals are saying it makes them feel unsafe. This happens as an active genocide continues in Gaza, with Israel calling upon 60,000 IDF reservists in preparation for the planned ethnic cleansing of a million civilians from Gaza City.

Whenever you see the western press centering the feelings of western Jews with extreme aggression, it's a safe bet that Israel has something especially ugly in the works.

•

The plan has always been to pace us from

"It's a complicated conflict and Hamas attacked on October 7 and gosh you sure are obsessed with Jews,"

to

"Well it's too late to do anything about it now,"

to

"Oh come on Gaza was so long ago and there's nothing we can do to change the past."

It really seems to have taken the empire by surprise that the public has not played along with this. They really expected us to forget about Gaza within the first few weeks and let it fade into the background. The fact that the outcry has only gotten louder says encouraging things about ordinary members of the public, and about the future of the human species. •

Zionism Is What It Does
•Notes From The Edge Of The Narrative Matrix•

Israel apologists always attack anti-Zionists by saying "Zionism just means self-determination for Jews! If you hate Zionism then you hate Jews!"

No, that's not what Zionism means. Zionism means exactly what we see before us today. Genocide. Ethnic cleansing. Apartheid. Nonstop violence and abuse. That's what Zionism means. And anti-Zionism means opposing these things.

There is simply no argument to the contrary. This is indisputably what Zionism looks like. There is no other alternate reality iteration of Zionism you can point to where genocide, ethnic cleansing, apartheid and nonstop violence and abuse are not happening. This is the only way Zionism looks. The Zionist experiment has been run, and these are the results.

Trying to argue that Zionism doesn't mean genocide, ethnic cleansing, apartheid, and nonstop violence and abuse is exactly the same as trying to argue that Nazism doesn't mean all the things that happened when the Nazism experiment was run. Nazism means all the things that happened under Nazism. You can't legitimately tell me "No, actually, Nazism just means a safe and prosperous homeland for the German people." We've seen what Nazism looks like, and we've seen what Zionism looks like. To argue otherwise is to argue with reality.

It's just so obnoxious how Israel supporters are like "Zionism means these nice things and nice words, so if you're against Zionism you're against the nice things and nice words!" No, asshole, that's not how it works. You're entitled to your own opinion, but not your own reality.

Israel is what it does. Zionism is what it does. You can't separate them from their actions. The debate about the true nature of these things has been settled by the reality of what is happening.

It doesn't matter if you believe Israel just wants to live in peace. It doesn't matter if you believe Zionism is just the idea that Jews deserve self-determination. Reality says you're wrong. Reality says Israel and Zionism mean nonstop violence and abuse. Reality says Israel and Zionism necessarily entail genocide, apartheid and ethnic cleansing. Because that's the reality on the ground.

Them's the facts. If you disagree with them, you are objectively wrong.

•

I saw a clip of ABC host Patricia Karvelas raking Netanyahu policy advisor Ophir Falk over the coals for his denialism of Israel's atrocities in Gaza, and the thought occurred to me that Israel really has lost the normies. All the mainstream western empire loyalists who dutifully toe the imperial line under normal circumstances are dropping away, one by one.

The fact that Israel has managed to alienate western liberals is so funny, because they'd be Israel's biggest cheerleaders if they were given the tiniest bit of justification for that position.

So much about Israel fits in perfectly with western liberal mythology. A US-aligned capitalist democracy run by a plucky religious minority who survived horrific persecution, which embraces secular progressive values and reinforces the dominant western narratives about the wonderful things the US-led order has been able to accomplish since its triumphant glorious victory in the second world war. All Israel had to do was give them something, anything, and they'd still think Israel is the greatest thing in the world. They just needed an excuse — even a very meager one.

But Israel couldn't even give them

that. Genocide, racism, apartheid, ethnic cleansing and expansionism were just too important to its driving ideology. The Zionist project simply could not continue without going mask-off at some point, so now they've lost all the mainstream moderate liberals and pretty much everyone besides the "killing Muslims is good" far right extremists and the "we have to support Israel because God commands it" Christian Zionists.

Eventually all the contradictions had to come out into the light.

•

The Israeli press are pushing the narrative that if people in Gaza are suffering so bad they should leave, which is precisely the narrative I said we'd soon be hearing from Israel in facilitation of its longstanding ethnic cleansing agenda.

Last month I wrote the following in an article titled "They're Starving Civilians To Steal A Palestinian Territory, And They're Lying About It":

"Western governments are beginning to speak out against the mass atrocity in Gaza, far too little and far too late. We can expect Israel and the United States to respond to this outcry by saying that Palestinians need to be evacuated out of Gaza as quickly as possible in order to rescue them from this deliberately manufactured humanitarian crisis. We can expect them to denounce anyone who opposes this ethnic cleansing operation as evil monsters who want to starve the poor Palestinians."

The Jerusalem Post has just published an opinion piece titled "Gaza humanitarian crisis should expedite Trump's relocation plan," subtitled "Now that there is public awareness of a humanitarian crisis in Gaza, it should be leveraged to garner support for Trump's Gaza relocation proposal."

The article's author, Gol Kalev, complains that "the Gazans" are being "denied the basic human right to flee a war" by the mean, nasty Europeans who just want to accuse Israel of war crimes and atrocities.

"They are needed under the rubble in Gaza — not just by Hamas, who uses them as human shields, but also by Europe and its proxies, who use them as pawns in their age-old opposition to the Jewish state, and as a proxy assault on America," Kalev writes, arguing that public frustration "should not be directed at Israel, but at those standing in the way of Trump's relocation plan, including European leaders."

"Now that there is public awareness of a humanitarian crisis in Gaza, it should be leveraged to garner support for Trump's Gaza relocation proposal — which could lead to safety and prosperity for Gazans, and peace for the entire region," writes Kalev. "The public message must be clear: Let the Gazans be free — let them flee."

Just as I said they would do, they're disguising a naked ethnic cleansing operation as humanitarianism and denouncing anyone who wants to provide Palestinians with a massive relief effort in their historic homeland as an uncaring monster. We can expect to see more of this messaging going forward.

•

Anyone who tells you they support Israel for religious reasons is telling you to stop trying to reason with them. They're saying their position is not based on facts, evidence, logic or morality, but their blind faith in a collection of made up stories. So there's nothing you could possibly say to them that would change their mind or convince them that they are wrong.

Trying to debate or reason with such a person would be the same as trying to convince someone that there is no God. It's an entirely unfalsifiable position about which no argument can be made using facts and evidence.

Someone like Mike Huckabee is never telling the truth or saying what he really thinks is going on when it comes to Israel and the Palestinians, he's just making whatever mouth noises he needs to make to help fulfill a Biblical prophecy and secure his eternal reward. Such people have no place in the conversation. They should be completely excluded from the debate, because they are not actually participating in it. They're just lying and manipulating for reasons that have nothing to do with truth or morality. •

"Why Doesn't Hamas Release The Hostages?", And Other Reader Questions

Nick on Patreon asks, "I don't know if this is a question that you would know the answer to, but it's worth a try. The one Zionist question I have a hard time answering is 'why don't Hamas release the hostages?' Israel doesn't give a shit about killing its own citizens, so they don't seem to be much of a bargaining chip."

The most important thing to make clear here is that anyone who suggests that Israel's onslaught in Gaza has anything whatsoever to do with hostages is either ignorant or lying. Netanyahu has explicitly said that Israel's attack will not end until Trump's ethnic cleansing plan to permanently remove all Palestinians from the Gaza Strip has been accomplished. This is not about freeing hostages, this is about a land grab that Israel has been pursuing for generations.

So when people say "why don't Hamas release the hostages?" in response to criticisms of Israel's genocidal atrocities in Gaza, they're generally just throwing up a completely fallacious red herring to nullify that criticism.

It is of course true that the Israeli government doesn't care about the hostages, but it's not accurate to say the hostages aren't a bargaining chip. Some 2.5 million Israelis are estimated to have filled the streets this past Sunday demanding that their government secure a deal to release the hostages — that's a quarter of the nation's population. Numbers like that amount to political pressure, even if the Netanyahu regime itself only cares about the land grab. They're not protesting because they care about stopping a genocide, they're doing it because they care about their own.

And of course the argument can be made that taking hostages is illegal and immoral under any circumstances, but most people tend to lose interest in this argument when they learn that thousands of Palestinian political prisoners are held captive by Israel without charge or trial as a matter of longstanding Israeli policy. You can argue that two wrongs don't make a right if you want, but it's hard to deny that Israel looks pretty ridiculous demanding the unconditional release of its hostages while holding thousands of Palestinians hostage itself. Everything Hamas has done to Israel are things Israel has been doing to Palestinians for decades at a far greater scale. When you do nasty things to people, you leave yourself open to retaliation in kind.

•

Elizabeth on Twitter asks, "Who are the journalists you read and admire?"

Too many to list. Some favorites include Julian Assange, Bisan Owda and everyone in Gaza who's ever taken a photo or made a video since 2023, the late great John Pilger, Chris Hedges, Joe Lauria and the folks at Consortium News, Dave DeCamp and everyone at Antiwar, Ali Abunimah and Asa Winstanley and everyone at Electronic Intifada, Aaron Maté and Max Blumenthal and everyone at The Grayzone, Rania Khalek and everyone at BreakThrough News, Ryan Grim and everyone at Drop Site News, Seymour Hersh, Glenn Greenwald, Muhammad Shehada, Amanda Yee, that anonymous Zei Squirrel account on Twitter, Alan MacLeod, Mark Ames, Yasha Levine, Kevin Gosztola, Sharmine Narwani, Arnaud Bertrand, Jonathan Cook, the Davids at Media Lens, and the Moon of Alabama blog.

•

Jo on Substack asks, "Hi Caitlin and Tim, apologies if you'd answered this before. You both write on here and I think i can detect a difference in tone and could hazard a guess as to which is which! I'm sure you agree on the big things; however, there must be things that you disagree on. How does this inform your work?"

Not really, to be honest. We have too much in common and were both raised to be critical of the US war machine, me by my journalist father and Tim by his Quaker upbringing. When we first got together Tim was sympathetic to American libertarianism, but I'd converted him into a godless commie using my womanly wiles before we started writing together.

We don't really disagree on anything political, or actually on much of anything these days. We used to have fights and arguments sometimes, but we don't really anymore. Our thing thrives on collaborative "yes, and"ing and mutual cheerleading; we're always trying to encourage each other and lift each other up.

Some people's idea of a happy couple looks like debate and healthy competition and keeping each other in check, but that sort of model has never worked for us. Ever since we got together we've had this urge to merge into each other and become one, and we've been getting closer and closer ever since we got together.

•

Buddhadev asks on Facebook, "You've said often that your hope for humanity lies in consciousness raising and spiritual awakening. I used believe this but no longer do. I know some incredibly experienced meditators, ayahuasca psychonauts, yogis/yoginis, etc who are ardent defenders of the Narrative Managers' takes on RussiaGate, Russia/ Ukraine, etc. On Gaza, many of them echo your 'favorite' corporate lib take wherein they talk about it as uncaused 'heartbreaking tragedy' that has no culprit behind it. Years of meeting people like this in 'hippie woo woo' communities (crystals, tarot, astrology, reikki, psychedelics, etc) has disabused me of any notion that their capacity for discernment is that much better than the general population. If you disagree and still think spiritual practice or consciousness expansion is the hope for ending war and tyranny, then what does such consciousness and spirituality look like to you and what should people be doing?"

There's not really any connection between being a good meditator/ yogini/psychonaut etc and a proper awakening, which is best understood as a radical shift in identity. People who wake up will often have spent time doing those things, but you can easily meditate your whole life without experiencing such a shift, and many have.

Some of the most toxic, unconscious, totally-asleep-at-the-wheel individuals I've ever encountered have had highly spiritual personalities.

Spiritual people are very often neurotic and miserable psychological train wrecks, because miserable people often turn to spirituality out of desperation to escape their suffering. Awakening isn't about having a particular kind of personality or becoming accomplished in a particular kind of spiritual practice — the illusion of the self who would be doing those things is precisely what's awakened from.

Awakening from the dream of selfing brings with it a drastic change in the human organism's relationship with mental narrative. Thoughts are no longer seen as true facts which need to be believed but as mental noises or energies which don't require our attention. From there thought takes on the role as a useful tool that can be picked up when it's needed and set down when it's not, rather than the writer, director and star of the whole show.

This has obvious implications for seeing through the veil of propaganda. You're much more aware of how dominated human consciousness is by mental narrative, and how much effort humans put into manipulating the narratives that other humans hold in their minds. Since thoughts don't demand belief like they used to, a narrative like "That Evil Dictator needs to be removed!" is a lot less likely to be uncritically taken on board.

That said, you can also have a powerful and authentic awakening without having a lucid understanding of what's really going on in the world. If 100 percent of your attention has gone into expanding your awareness of your internal processes, then you haven't been putting any effort into expanding your awareness of what's going on in the outer world. This is why you'll sometimes see relatively awake people regurgitating the CNN line on a given issue; they simply haven't yet put the effort into expanding their consciousness in that direction.

You can be spiritually enlightened while remaining clueless about Palestine in the same way you can be clear on Palestine while remaining totally transfixed by egoic delusion; the call is to expand consciousness both inwardly and outwardly. A sufficiently clear awakening will bring with it a call to compassion and a deep caring about the plight of humanity, which will naturally give rise to a curiosity about what factors are driving all the dysfunction we see in our society today. In the information age it's not hard for that impulse to translate into a lucid perception of the abusive systems and power structures which are driving our species to its doom.

And really to talk about it as "inward" and "outward" isn't quite accurate. Past a certain point of clarification you start to notice that all the dysfunction you see in the world is mirrored in the dysfunctionality you've found in yourself. You can see the Israel in you. The empire in you. The war profiteer in you. The propagandist in you. You no longer see yourself as separate from the wrongs of the world, and you just set about working to heal them wherever you see them — whether it's in your own psyche or in a bombing campaign overseas. They're not separate things.

So you're right, a simple entry-level awakening won't be enough to save us. We've got to become a truly conscious species by awakening to reality in all the ways that are relevant to the human adventure. •

Only Liars And Manipulators Say Israel Isn't Starving Gaza

Israeli news outlet Haaretz has published a harrowing report on starvation in Gaza which further discredits the Israeli narrative that the photos of skeletal children we've been seeing are antisemitic Hamas propaganda, for anyone who's still clinging to delusions about such things.

Haaretz reporters were taken by doctors on video tours of hospitals in Gaza, conducting interviews with numerous medical personnel and obtaining many photos of civilians showing signs of extreme starvation. Throughout the report we encounter story after story of severely emaciated children, mothers unable to breastfeed starving babies because of their own starvation, people with preexisting conditions severely exacerbated by malnutrition, diseases spreading due to crippled healthcare infrastructure and ruined immune systems, and wounds failing to heal due to inadequate food intake.

The article is one of the more uncomfortable things I've seen throughout the entirety of this genocide, and that's saying something.

"What we saw there left no room for doubt about the scale of the horror," write Haaretz reporters Yarden Michaeli and Nir Hasson.

"Seventeen youngsters had deteriorated into a state of severe malnutrition without preexisting health conditions; 10 suffered from previous illnesses," they write, saying "Anyone who claims that the images of starvation in the Gaza Strip are a result of acute genetic or other diseases, and not due to a grave shortage of food, are lying to themselves."

This comes as the UN-backed Integrated Food Security Phase Classification (IPC) formally declares that the people of Gaza are suffering from a famine that "is entirely man-made", which must be halted and reversed with extreme urgency.

Israel has of course denounced the IPC's findings as antisemitic Hamas propaganda, with the Israeli Foreign Ministry saying that "The entire IPC document is based on Hamas lies laundered through organizations with vested interests," and Benjamin Netanyahu branding the report "a modern blood libel, spreading like wildfire through prejudice."

You might find this response ridiculous, and of course it is, but really, what else does Israel have left? When all major human rights institutions are accusing you of horrific crimes, your only options are either (A) admit the obvious fact that there's no way every single mainstream humanitarian organization is lying about your actions, or (B) claim that they're all in on a giant globe-spanning conspiracy because of a nefarious prejudice against your religion.

Of course they're going to go with (B). This is Israel we're talking about, after all.

When a nation keeps having to publish denials that it is intentionally starving civilians, you can safely assume it's because that nation is intentionally starving civilians. If you saw someone on social media loudly denying the latest allegations that they are a child molester over and over again for two years, you probably wouldn't let them babysit your kids.

I have never once felt the need to publish a denial that I am intentionally starving people, because I have never intentionally starved anyone. It's not something I've ever found myself needing to say even one time, let alone many many times constantly.

You don't see the government of Ireland constantly denying that Ireland is intentionally starving civilians, because Ireland is not intentionally starving civilians.

You don't see pro-China spinmeisters frantically churning out propaganda denying that China is intentionally starving civilians, because China is not intentionally starving civilians.

You don't see Brazilian internet trolls aggressively swarming the comments of anyone who says Brazil is intentionally starving civilians,

because Brazil is not intentionally starving civilians.

You don't see the Pakistani government paying social media influencers to assert on their platforms that Pakistan is not intentionally starving civilians, because Pakistan is not intentionally starving civilians.

You see an intense campaign of narrative management aimed at denying that Israel has been intentionally starving civilians because Israel is intentionally starving civilians. That's why all the constant government denials, the endless propaganda and spin pieces and PR stunts, and relentless online trolling operations have been necessary.

Most Israel apologia at this point is just people pretending to believe things they don't really believe. Palestinians aren't really being starved. Gaza looks like a gravel parking lot because Hamas put explosives in all the buildings. The IDF has a low civilian-to-combatant kill ratio. Gaza's entire healthcare infrastructure was destroyed because Hamas was hiding under all the hospitals. Nobody actually believes these things. They're just pretending to believe them in order to justify genocidal atrocities and help ensure that they continue.

They're really the worst people in the world. •

Never Forget The Lies They Told About Gaza. Never Forgive Them.
•Notes From The Edge Of The Narrative Matrix•

A joint investigation by The Guardian and +972 Magazine found that the IDF's own records show that civilians make up at least 83 percent of those killed in Israeli attacks on Gaza. The report notes that the real number is likely significantly higher, since the number given doesn't include the thousands upon thousands of dead civilians who are still unaccounted for in Gaza because they are trapped under the rubble, or those killed by indirect means such as starvation or disease.

The pro-Israel spin machine frantically tried to discredit this report as soon as it came out, but their arguments have been soundly debunked.

They claimed that Israel has a phenomenally low civilian-to-combatant casualty ratio, then Israel's own data proved that civilians comprise the vast majority of those killed by the IDF.

They denied that Israel is starving Gaza, then the IPC came out with a report saying that Israel is starving Gaza.

They tried to claim that the skeletal children we're seeing in Gaza looked that way because of pre-existing conditions, then the Israeli press published an extensive report showing that children with no pre-existing conditions are being starved.

They tried to deny that Israeli soldiers were massacring civilians at aid sites, then the Israeli soldiers themselves told the Israeli press that they were being ordered to massacre civilians at aid sites.

Never forget all the monsters who tried to gaslight you and convince you that you are crazy and hateful for saying these things are happening. Never, ever forgive them.

•

The IDF has admitted to uprooting thousands of olive trees in the West Bank on Thursday. The routine destruction of Palestinian olive trees is not the most shocking or evil thing that Israel does to the Palestinians, but it does speak to what its true intentions are in a unique way.

Similar to the way white people killed off all the bison to help eliminate the American Indians, killing olive trees deprives Palestinians of an important means of earning a living, and strikes at an important aspect of Palestinian identity and culture.

Olive trees can live for thousands of years; people with a strong attachment to the land treasure and protect them, while the Israelis who claim to be "indigenous" to the area are destroying them and replacing them with highly flammable foreign plants. You can tell who the actual indigenous population is by watching their behavior.

•

Normal person: Genocide is bad

Crazy person: Woah hey, let's not get political

•

Right wingers are like "No no you don't understand, Israel is protecting western civilization. If we don't help Israel genocide the Palestinians and starve their children and burn their babies and bomb their hospitals and demolish their cities, one day we could wind up ruled by evil murderous savages."

•

Normal person: Oh no those people over there are committing genocide!

Crazy person: Okay but what religion are they?

•

The way Zionists talk about Palestinian hatred of Jews you'd think the Palestinians immigrated to Israel from somewhere else in 1948 in order to attack Jewish people.

•

In 1937, Winston Churchill stated the following while arguing in favor of allowing Jews to settle in Palestine:

"I do not admit that the dog in the manger has the final right to the manger, even though he may have lain there for a very long time. I do not admit that right. I do not admit, for instance, that a great wrong has been done to the Red Indians of America, or the black people of Australia. I do not admit that a wrong has been done to those people by the fact that a stronger race, a higher-grade race, or, at any rate, a more worldly-wise race, to put it that way, has come in and taken their place. I do not admit it. I do not think the Red Indians had any right to say, The American Continent belongs to us and we are not going to have any of these European settlers coming in here. They had not the right, nor had they the power."

Churchill knew exactly what he was looking at in the Zionist agenda to colonize Palestine. There was no confusion whatsoever. It wasn't until much later that history was revised through propaganda to spin this as something other than the western settler-colonialist project that it has always been.

•

The other day I wrote the following in a rant about religious Zionists:

"Someone like Mike Huckabee is never telling the truth or saying what he really thinks is going on when it comes to Israel and the Palestinians, he's just making whatever mouth noises he needs to make to help fulfill a Biblical prophecy and secure his eternal reward. Such people have no place in the conversation. They should be completely excluded from the debate, because they are not actually participating in it. They're just lying and manipulating for reasons that have nothing to do with truth or morality."

The very next day, Antiwar published an article titled "Mike Huckabee Claims Israeli Settlements in the Occupied West Bank Are Not Illegal Under International Law".

Like I said. Huckabee does not believe this obvious falsehood, he's just saying whatever words he needs to say to help advance the agendas of his weird Christian cult. These freaks consider themselves so pious and righteous, but in reality they are some of the most conniving, unethical deceivers our world has ever seen.

•

It just occurred to me that at some point in the future they're going to try to demand that we condemn whatever radicalized groups and militias wind up emerging as a result of the Gaza genocide.

That's gonna be cute. •

"Is Hamas Causing The Famine?", And Other Reader Questions

Silvia asks on Facebook, "Many people in Europe are convinced that the famine in Gaza is caused by Hamas stealing humanitarian supplies. Where is the truth?"

The truth is that this is a propaganda narrative which has been debunked by some of the most pro-Israel, pro-establishment sources you can imagine. The New York Times reported last month that senior Israeli military officials had said this is false:

> "For nearly two years, Israel has accused Hamas of stealing aid provided by the United Nations and other international organizations. The government has used that claim as its main rationale for restricting food from entering Gaza.

> "But the Israeli military never found proof that the Palestinian militant group had systematically stolen aid from the United Nations, the biggest supplier of emergency assistance to Gaza for most of the war, according to two senior Israeli military officials and two other Israelis involved in the matter."

Also last month, Reuters reported the following:

> "An internal U.S. government analysis found no evidence of systematic theft by the Palestinian militant group Hamas of U.S.-funded humanitarian supplies, challenging the main rationale that Israel and the U.S. give for backing a new armed private aid operation.

> "The analysis, which has not been previously reported, was conducted by a bureau within the U.S. Agency for International Development and completed in late June. It examined 156 incidents of theft or loss of U.S.-funded supplies reported by U.S. aid partner organizations between October 2023 and this May."

These are mainstream media sources citing Israeli military officials and the US government, respectively. This claim could not be more thoroughly debunked than it is, and it's insane that I still see people trying to push it.

Every major human rights group is in agreement that people in Gaza are starving because Israel is starving them, from Doctors Without Borders to Amnesty International to Human Rights Watch to UN special rapporteurs to hundreds of NGOs. This is a settled matter.

•

We Are The Many, They Are The Few on Twitter asks, "A question, how do you see yourself politically? You've mentioned you're not a Marxist, but you do seem close to it."

The best way I've been able to sum up my politics is that I support shoving things as far to the left as possible until we get a healthy world. Shoving as far away from capitalism, ecocide, militarism, empire-building, oppression and exploitation as is necessary to have a peaceful and harmonious world where everyone gets what they need and we're not cannibalizing our biosphere for shareholder profits.

I probably am pretty close to a Marxist in a lot of ways, but I avoid categorizing myself as such for a couple of personal reasons which are unlikely to be of interest to many people.

Firstly, I try to avoid joining up with any ideological factions because humanity is still in a state of extreme delusion at present, so even the best political groups will be full of wildly dysfunctional individuals whose thinking and behavior I'd rather keep at arm's length to make sure I stay on the right track. I'll help with leftist movements and agendas where I can be of service in my own capacity like I am with Palestine right now, but I personally don't find that aligning myself with any group is a safe move at this point in the human adventure.

Secondly I try to avoid limiting my thinking to anyone else's -ists or -isms. I've seen a lot of Marxists get super religious about it and close themselves off to whole aspects of human psychology and spirituality just because of something some dead guy said in the 1880s. That's something I find too confining as a writer, as a thinker, and as a human organism.

•

Teddy on Substack asks, "Your paintings absolutely rival your writing. Have you had formal art training or are you a self discovered painter?"

Art was my best subject in school and I've always enjoyed it, but I never really buckled down and pursued it in a disciplined way until Covid when I taught myself oil painting through some online courses. Before that I mostly did watercolor, block printing, and drawing.

•

misschryss on Twitter asks, "Where do you find the time to write so prolifically? And do you ever use AI to help you write? How do you make a living?"

I'm fortunate enough to be an entirely reader-funded writer, with many small donors supporting this project so that I and my husband/cowriter can work at this thing full-time.

I have never used AI to help me write, and I never will. I honestly don't believe AI will ever be able to do what I do, because so much of it comes from inspiration and insight that machines will never be able to imitate.

With regard to staying prolific (major overshare incoming), one indispensable tool is maintaining high sexual energy. Men can train themselves to orgasm without ejaculating, allowing a high level of sexual energy to be maintained at all times which two partners can then keep stoked in each other with mutual attraction. This allows for a fairly stable state of inspiration and creative output where your intense attraction to each other turns you both into each other's muse.

•

The Revolution Continues asks on Substack, "Question for Caitlin and Tim: What is your writing process like? Do you come up with ideas for a piece separately and write the article separately, then come together and discuss and revise together or is the opposite — you write and discuss together and then separately revise? Thanks for letting us take a look into your heads!"

The only thing I do separately from Tim in this project is the painting; the writing is intimately collaborative. Articles typically start with a conversation where one of us says something interesting or insightful, and we unpack it verbally before turning it into text. The sparkliest lines you'll read here are usually a repetition of something we'd said out loud to each other not long before, often verbatim.

We live and work joined at the hip; we're both writers and we enjoy writing, but one of the main reasons we love this job so much is because it has allowed us to be together every day. We had a long-distance relationship from 2014 to 2016 before Tim came to Australia from the US, and ever since we've been together we've avoided spending any time apart. Being separate that whole time was excruciating, but it really made us appreciate how much we like being near each other.

In terms of what our individual roles are, I'm more of the big-picture guiding vision for the overall spirit and direction of the project, and Tim's better at the details. One way of describing it is that what we write is more Caitlin, how it's written is more Tim. The general mood, ideology, content and character of these writings is more Caitlin, but that one liner or crackling bit of prose that stuck in your memory is more likely to have come from Tim. But there's extensive overlap in both of those areas too. Like I said, it's intimately collaborative. •

Those Who Condemn Hamas Lack Empathy And Humility

Whenever I see someone going out of their way to denounce the Palestinian resistance while expressing some vaguely pro-Palestine sentiment, I take it as an admission that they aren't capable of basic human empathy. They look at October 7 and think "I can't imagine myself doing that," and conclude from this that the perpetrators of October 7 must be worse people than they are.

They stop their examination there. They never ask themselves what it would have been like to live the life of a young man who ended up joining Hamas. They never ask themselves what it would have been like to live one's entire life in a giant concentration camp under the thumb a genocidal apartheid state which routinely murders and abuses your countrymen. They simply look at the actions of October 7 from the prism of their own experience as a comfortable western suburbanite on the other side of the world and think, "I would never conduct such an attack; I am much too virtuous and compassionate."

No you're just too comfortable and coddled, and you're too much of an emotional infant to consciously put yourself in someone else's shoes. Any one of us who lived their life in Gaza would have experienced the effects of the tyranny and abusiveness of the Israeli regime, and our worldview would have been shaped accordingly. You would come to hate those who hate you. If they were sufficiently abusive toward you and your loved ones, at some point you would probably experience the desire to return some of the violence your people have been receiving.

This would not make you a bad person. It would not mean that you are less moral or righteous than some white westerner sitting on their couch condemning Hamas on social media between mouthfuls of doritos. It would simply mean you were shaped by the conditions of your life, just like everyone else.

You can understand Israeli violence using the exact same empathy tools, by the way. Rather than viewing Israelis as innocent little victims responding defensively to unprovoked attacks by murderous savages, or doing the opposite and viewing Jewish people as an inherently wicked race, you can simply ask yourself what it would be like to grow up in an apartheid state whose existence depends on dehumanizing those who don't belong to the group which that state empowers.

How would it shape you to be raised in a very young ethnostate which was dropped on top of a pre-existing civilization whose people never accepted that they ought to be displaced, deprived of basic rights, and live as a permanent lower caste just because they're a different ethnicity? How would your mind and conscience be formed if you were indoctrinated from a very young age to believe there's a perfectly good reason why you're living a much better life than the people in that other group, and that the reason is because the other group is inherently inferior to yours? How would the formation of your worldview play out if you were always being told that you're surrounded by mindless barbarians who want to kill you because of your religion and can only be brought to heel by brute force?

If you think you'd be any better than the average Israeli after such an upbringing, you're fooling yourself. With a little empathy and humility you can understand that both the Israelis and the Palestinians are conditioned in different ways by the circumstances of their lives and the systems under which they live.

The existence of this inherently racist and tyrannical state shapes everyone who lives under it. The creation of a state which cannot be sustained without nonstop violence and abuse was always going to give rise to hatred, trauma and enmity. We were always headed for this point.

Between the Palestinians and the Israelis there is a very clear victim and a very clear victimizer, but that's not because anyone involved is inherently evil. It's egoically comfortable to sit on our high horse and see Virtuous Good Guys over here and Villainous Bad Guys over there, but real life doesn't work that way. In real life,

any of us could have been Hamas, and any of us could have been a genocidal IDF soldier. If you can't see this, it's because you lack empathy and humility. That's a character flaw, and you should do what you can to change that about yourself.

As with so much else, it's not about the individuals, it's about the system. The unjust system upon which the Zionist state is based has proved beyond a shadow of a doubt that it can never exist without nonstop violence and abuse, so that system needs to be dismantled and replaced with something radically different, just as was the case with Nazi Germany and apartheid South Africa. And just as was the case with Nazi Germany and apartheid South Africa, external pressures will probably need to play a role in forcing that change to take place.

That's the only way forward. That's the only way there can be peace. •

21 Questions About The Claim That Iran Orchestrated Antisemitic Attacks In Australia

Australian prime minister Anthony Albanese has announced that Canberra will be expelling the Iranian ambassador and legislating to list Iran's Islamic Revolutionary Guard Corps as a terrorist group. Albanese says the move is because an assessment by the intelligence agency ASIO has concluded that Iran used a "complex web of proxies" to orchestrate two antisemitic arson attacks in Australia in order to "undermine social cohesion and sow discord".

As you might expect, not one shred of evidence has been provided for this assertion, much less the giant mountain of rock-solid proof required for intelligence agency credibility in a post-Iraq invasion world.

This hasn't stopped the Murdoch press from going ballistic and framing the assertion as a "bombshell revelation" of an established fact. It also hasn't stopped Australia's state broadcaster the ABC from publishing an article by Laura Tingle with the flagrantly propagandistic title "Revelations Iran was behind antisemitic attacks show IRGC tentacles have reached Australia". Evidence-free assertions made by the government are not "revelations", and

to frame them as such is journalistic malpractice.

The Israeli government has publicly claimed credit for pressuring Albanese to take these actions, after Netanyahu personally inserted himself into Australian affairs by repeatedly publicly expressing outrage about alleged antisemitic incidents in Australia.

Anyway, here are 21 questions we should all be asking about these new claims:

1. Where is the evidence?

2. May we please see the evidence?

3. Why can't we see the evidence?

4. In what way would it benefit Iran to orchestrate antisemitic attacks in Australia?

5. In what way would it benefit Iran to "undermine social cohesion and sow discord" in Australia?

6. Please explain how orchestrating antisemitic attacks in Australia would advance Iranian interests more than the interests of some other state, like, say, just for example, Israel?

7. What foreign intelligence agencies were involved in helping ASIO gather the information it used to make its assessment about the Iranian involvement in these incidents?

8. What were the names of all the people in the "complex web of

proxies" allegedly used to conduct these attacks which ASIO claims ultimately traced back to Tehran?

9. Does Anthony Albanese's announcement that Iran is staging antisemitic attacks in Australia have anything to do with Benjamin Netanyahu's stern letter to Albanese a week earlier demanding that the prime minister take action on alleged antisemitic incidents in Australia by the deadline of September 23?

10. Does Albanese's announcement that Iran is staging antisemitic attacks in Australia have anything to do with the fact that Israel is reportedly very close to initiating another war with Iran?

11. Does Albanese's announcement that Iran is staging antisemitic attacks in Australia have anything to do with the way Australians have been filling the streets in massive numbers to protest the Gaza holocaust?

12. Why kick out the Iranian ambassador and designate the IRGC as a terrorist group while keeping the Israeli ambassador in Australia and doing absolutely nothing to stop the IDF during an active genocide?

13. Which state benefits more from the Australian government's efforts to stomp out free speech in the name of curbing antisemitic incidents: Iran or Israel?

14. Which state would benefit more from fomenting hostilities between Canberra and Tehran: Iran or Israel?

15. Are we being asked to forget the way Australian intelligence services facilitated the lies that led to the invasion of Iraq, or simply to ignore this?

16. Are we being asked to forget the fact that we've been lied to and manipulated about all things involving Israel for the last two years, or simply to ignore this?

17. Are we being asked to forget that the claims about "antisemitic attacks" in Australia have been exposed as bogus or riddled with glaring plot holes over and over again since 2023, or simply to ignore this?

18. Are we being asked to forget that supporters of Israel have an extensive history of staging false antisemitic incidents in order to advance the interests of the Zionist state, or simply to ignore this?

19. Does the Australian government believe Australians are all complete slobbering idiots?

2o. Does the Australian government believe Australians are all high on ayahuasca?

21. What specific mental illness, intellectual disability, or chemically-induced altered state of consciousness does the Australian government believe Australians are all suffering from which would cause us to accept these unfounded assertions as true?

Of course none of these questions will ever be answered by anyone with real power. The reason it's ASIO telling us this happened instead of police or investigative journalists is because police and journalists are expected to lay out the evidence for their assertions, while intelligence agencies are not.

Whenever the powerful present us with evidence-free incendiary claims of significant consequence, I like to remind my readers of Hitchens' razor: "What can be asserted without evidence can also be dismissed without evidence."

It sure was selfless of the Iranians to orchestrate these attacks against their own interests, solely to benefit the interests of Israel, just as hundreds of thousand of Australians are filling the streets in protest against Israel's genocidal atrocities, and just as Israel prepares for war with Iran. That sure was kind and charitable of them.

Bunch of top blokes, those Iranians. It's too bad they're terrorists now.

"The Arabs Hate Us Because Of Our Religion" Is The New "They Hate Us For Our Freedom"
•Notes From The Edge Of The Narrative Matrix•

Israelis who say "the Arabs hate us because of our religion" are as self-evidently moronic as the Americans who said "they hate us for our freedom". In both cases the answer is no, dipshit, they hate you because of the horrific things to do to them.

•

Western leaders who say they'll recognize a Palestinian state while feebly calling on Both Sides to reach a ceasefire deal are just cuter, more photogenic versions of Netanyahu. They're making empty noises to appear as though they're doing something while refusing to actually lift a finger to stop the genocide.

They know Israel's not going to make a permanent ceasefire deal because Netanyahu has explicitly stated that the slaughter won't end until the ethnic cleansing of Gaza is complete. That's why Tel Aviv is just ignoring the fact that Hamas agreed to a ceasefire a week and a half ago; there is absolutely nothing Hamas could agree to which would stop Israel from doing everything it needs to do to steal a Palestinian territory from the Palestinians who live there. The assault on Gaza has never been about removing Hamas; it has always been about removing the Palestinians.

Western leaders are pretending not to know this and promoting the false notion that Israel is basically acting in good faith in these negotiations, and that the only obstacle is Israel and Hamas being unable to successfully agree to terms. Participating in this mass deception while refusing to take any concrete actions to end the genocide is participating in the genocide. They're not dropping the bombs or firing the bullets, but they're helping to make sure they keep raining death and destruction on Palestinians.

They are Netanyahu with a nice guy smile. They are good cop Netanyahu.

•

After the Australian government announced its ASIO-sourced conclusion that Iran had directed multiple antisemitic attacks in Australia in order to "undermine social cohesion and sow discord," I published a list of questions regarding the matter which included the following:

"7. What foreign intelligence agencies were involved in helping ASIO gather the information it used to make its assessment about the Iranian involvement in these incidents?"

Shortly thereafter, Sky News Australia ran a report titled "Sources reveal Israeli intelligence assisted ASIO investigation into Iran in major tip-off".

So I guess we can consider that question answered.

•

One of the reasons socialists don't focus on conspiracy analysis and the deep state as much as the right is because it's not our only argument. It's not that conspiracies and parapolitical power structures don't exist, they absolutely do, but because we're not ideologically compelled to make excuses for the unavoidable abuses of capitalism we don't need to act like any specific cabal of machiavellian elites is the source and summit of all our problems.

The rightist suffers from the delusion that capitalism would be working perfectly fine if a few nefarious individuals weren't scheming behind the scenes ruining the capitalism for everyone. The leftist recognizes that corruption, corporatism, inequality and domination are the inevitable products of a profit-driven system under which the capitalist class are able to exploit the working class who have nothing to sell but their labor. We therefore often find it less important to focus on the specifics of the way those abuses are playing out, because we understand that even if you eliminated all the current oligarchs and their secret plans and the strings they pull to manipulate the official government, if you didn't also replace our entire system with something radically different they'd be replaced by new oligarchic manipulators in short order.

For those who understand the inherently exploitative, ecocidal, unjust and violent nature of capitalism,

the strongest arguments against status quo power structures are not invisible conspiracies happening in secret, but the monstrous abuses that are happening right out in the open. The genocide in Gaza. Our dying biosphere. The fact that people struggle to keep a roof over their heads and put food on the table while others fly private jets to private islands paid for by the exploitation of thousands of impoverished workers. The fact that the most powerful country on earth doesn't have a real healthcare system. The fact that an empire-like alliance of western governments and their proxies keeps expanding its warmongering, militarism and nuclear brinkmanship around the world with the goal of complete planetary domination.

It is an indisputable fact that rich and powerful individuals conspire with each other to the detriment of ordinary people, and at times it can be useful to highlight who those individuals are and the things that they are doing. But the leftist sees people opening their eyes to these abuses as a means to an end, not as an end in itself. When the rightist spotlights those abuses it's to say "Look what these individuals are doing! If we just removed these individuals from power everything would be working fine!" When the leftist does so, it's to say "See these are the kinds of people who rise to the top under a system where human behavior is driven by the pursuit of profit, and profit is most readily

obtained through exploitation, injustice and ecocide. These kinds of people will always rule over us until we have replaced that system with a different one." •

Western Civilization Is Not Worth Saving

Western civilization is not worth saving. I think that's been pretty well established by now.

That's one of the silliest things about the way rightists are always babbling about how we need to protect our way of life from immigrants or Islam or "the trans agenda" or whatever. They're beginning with the assumption that this train wreck of a society is worth saving at all.

I am not saying that westerners should die. I am not saying that all the ideals and values that westerners purport to hold are worthless. I am saying that this civilization, as it actually exists, is an indefensible disaster. Clearly.

Our way of living on this planet. The way we treat one another. The way we treat people on other continents. All the systems and social structures that give rise to the way things are. These things should not exist. We should not be the way that we are.

This civilization is genocidal. Ecocidal. Omnicidal. Imperialist. Racist. Dehumanizing. Degrading. Dystopian. Emotionally stunted. Culturally vapid. Spiritually impoverished. Intellectually enslaved. Why would any sane person want this to continue?

We don't need to rescue western civilization from outside forces, we need to rescue ourselves from western civilization.

If we listen to our hearts we can understand that the call isn't to save western civilization from corruption by foreign cultures or new ways of thinking, but to radically transform it from the murderous, tyrannical and oppressive nightmare that it has always been.

The western way of life doesn't need to be preserved, it needs to end. We cannot keep doing this. We cannot go on this way. We cannot keep poisoning our planet, our minds, our hearts and our souls with the McGenocide ideology of the western empire. We are headed somewhere dark, somewhere none of us want to go, and we need to turn around.

Nothing about our old way of doing things has worked out for us. Everything we were doing before wound up bringing us to this terrible point. We don't need to go backwards, and we don't need to stay still. We need to evolve.

Gaza is a mirror. It's showing us what we are. What we have always been.

It's time to be real about what we are seeing. •

Dear Western Liberal,

Dear western liberal,

Saying "I support a two-state solution" does not release you from your moral obligation to ferociously oppose a genocide backed by your own government.

Saying "I oppose Netanyahu" does not release you from your moral obligation to ferociously oppose a genocide backed by your own government.

Saying you find the Gaza holocaust "heartbreaking" and "terrible" does not release you from your moral obligation to ferociously oppose a genocide backed by your own government.

Saying "I want there to be peace" does not release you from your moral obligation to ferociously oppose a genocide backed by your own government.

Saying you think "both sides" should cease their aggressions does not release you from your moral obligation to ferociously oppose a genocide backed by your own government.

Saying "it's complicated and I don't understand it" does not release you from your moral obligation to ferociously oppose a genocide backed by your own government.

Saying "Hamas attacked on October 7" does not release you from your moral obligation to ferociously oppose a genocide backed by your own government.

Saying "the Jews deserve a homeland" does not release you from your moral obligation to ferociously oppose a genocide backed by your own government.

Saying "I'm busy" does not release you from your moral obligation to ferociously oppose a genocide backed by your own government.

Saying "I'm overwhelmed" does not release you from your moral obligation to ferociously oppose a genocide backed by your own government.

We are all morally obligated to do everything we can to oppose a live-streamed genocide that's being facilitated, supported and defended by the western power structure under which we live. Nothing besides tooth-and-claw ferocious opposition satisfies that moral obligation.

Don't tell me about your feelings. Don't tell me what political positions you support. Don't tell me what thoughts you privately think to yourself. Do everything you can to stop the genocide that's being facilitated by your government and its allies.

Nothing else qualifies. Nothing else is defensible. Nothing else will satisfy the questions you'll be asked by younger generations about what you did during the Gaza holocaust. •

They're Lying About Venezuela While Moving War Machinery Into Place

As if we didn't have enough ugliness in the world right now, Trump has deployed warships near Venezuela's coast, prompting Caracas to ready drone and naval patrols for conflict.

In an article titled "Inside Trump's gunboat diplomacy with Venezuela," Axios' Marc Caputo writes that "The U.S. has never been closer to armed conflict with Venezuela, with a fully loaded U.S. flotilla sitting off its coast and dictator Nicolás Maduro living under a $50 million bounty."

"President Trump ordered seven warships carrying 4,500 personnel — including three guided-missile destroyers and at least one attack submarine — to the waters off Venezuela," Caputo writes. "Officially, they're there to combat drug trafficking. But Press Secretary Karoline Leavitt leaned into the ambiguity of the mission on Thursday, noting that the U.S. considers Maduro the 'fugitive head of [a] drug cartel' and not Venezuela's legitimate president."

The US personnel reportedly include some 2,200 Marines.

"This could be Noriega part 2," an unnamed official in the Trump administration told Axios, saying that "Maduro should be shitting bricks."

So they're not even disguising the fact that Trump is at least contemplating some kind of direct military strike on Caracas. Drugs are the official-official reason for the deployment, but the unofficial-official reason that's being freely leaked to the press is to remove the leader of a sovereign state.

It's probably worth noting that Trump-aligned pundits like Alex Jones have been busy manufacturing consent for regime change intervention in Venezuela.

"I don't like any of these wars," Jones said recently on whatever his show is called now. "But if you look at US doctrine and wars that we fought that were right, it's in Latin America, this is our sandbox. And Venezuela is a communist dictatorship with the biggest oil reserves per square foot in the world, their people are absolute slaves, and I don't like regime change, but they're manipulating our elections, they're flooding us with Fentanyl, and if there were surgical strikes to take out the communists there would be an uprising and they could have elections, and it would be a good thing."

Jones could have stopped at "communist" and "oil reserves". Venezuela has the largest proven oil reserves of any country on the planet, and is not aligned with the capitalist western empire that is loosely centralized around Washington DC. Any reasons given for US regime change intervention beyond this should be read as excuses.

Whenever the US war machine moves its crosshairs to a different target I always get people telling me "No no Caitlin, THIS time the Evil Bad Guy really DOES need to be regime changed! THIS time our government and media are telling us the TRUTH!"

And it's always so stupid, because it's just the same rehashed lies over and over again. The empire takes whatever actions will help it to dominate our planet and its resources to a greater extent than it already does, and then it makes up justifications for those actions.

They'll say they're doing it for humanitarian reasons while ignoring the humanitarian abuses of empire-aligned nations. They'll say they're doing it to stop drug abuse while ignoring all the evidence regarding the actual causes of drug abuse, even as Maduro sends 15,000 troops to the Colombian border to help fight drug trafficking. They'll say they're doing it to stop interference in US affairs while letting US-aligned nations like Israel interfere in US politics at will.

They're just lying. The US empire lies about all its acts of war. Trump tried to orchestrate a regime change in Venezuela the last time he was in office, and he's doing it again for the exact same reasons. It's an oil-rich nation that refuses to bow to the dictates of Washington, and all the worst warmongers in the imperial swamp are eagerly pushing to absorb it into the folds of the empire.

That's all we are looking at here, and anyone who says otherwise is lying. •

On Israel, Australia, And Racism

Israeli journalist Gideon Levy has a new article in Haaretz titled "Most of Israel's Protest Movement Only Cares About the Lives of the Gaza Hostages — Not of Palestinians" where he discusses his frustration and disgust with the massive disparity between the value his countrymen place on Israeli and Palestinian lives.

"They worry about the lives of 20 hostages while ignoring the fact that their country kills 20 innocent people an hour on average," Levy writes. "For them, humanity stops at the borders of nationality. They'll leave no stone unturned to help any Israeli but avert their gaze with a lack of interest in the case of a Palestinian whose fate is often much worse. They are enraged at Benjamin Netanyahu's cold-heartedness, but theirs is no less evident. When it comes to Palestinians, they exhibit the same evil and cold hearts."

"How can one be shocked at the sight of starving hostage Evyatar David and shrug or even rejoice at the killing taking place in lines for food?" askes Levy. "How can one be shocked at the murder of the Bibas family yet show no interest in the 1,000 babies and 19,000 children killed by the IDF, or in the 40,000 Gazan orphans? How can one lose sleep over Hamas tunnels and show no interest in what goes on at the Sde Teiman or Megiddo detention centers, to our shame? How is this possible?"

And, of course, we know how it's possible. It's possible because of racism. It's possible because Israelis see Palestinians as subhuman savages whose lives are worth far less than their own.

Levy acknowledges this further down in his piece:

"Viewing human beings — children, the disabled, the elderly, women, and other helpless people as dust, as people whose killing and starvation are legitimate, with their property worthless and their dignity non-existent — is tantamount to being Netanyahu, Ben-Gvir and Smotrich.

"Opposing total evil, one must stand for total humanity, which is almost non-existent in Israel."

This is why I always dismiss anyone who tries to defend Israel by citing its widespread protests. They're not protesting against the genocide, they're protesting because of Israeli captives and Israeli casualties. It's a shitty, racist society full of shitty, racist people.

I've been thinking about racism more than usual today because of the discourse around anti-immigrant protests this weekend here in Melbourne and around Australia, which were both full of violent neo-Nazis and numerous Israeli flags.

The Zionist institutions of Australia who've been shrieking their lungs out about pro-Palestine protests these last two years seem to be pretty chill about actual Nazis marching through their streets.

All the ugliest things about Australia are also the ugliest things about Israel, and our ugly things happen to get along swimmingly with theirs.

To be racist is to admit that you are a dull, vapid person. It's an admission that you are so intellectually, emotionally and spiritually shallow that you can only enjoy and connect with other human beings in the most superficial of ways. There is no depth to you. There has been no growth in you. You are stunted. You have been wasting your time on this planet instead of maturing and expanding your connectedness with the gift of human life.

If you have been growing and maturing, your ability to delight in other people isn't limited by skin color, culture, language, national background, or religion. You understand that there are whole universes within us beyond those few superficial differences, and we are able to connect with each other on all those various levels in a limitless number of ways. You don't fear and shun the differentness of others, you take immense enjoyment from it.

If you have not been growing and maturing, you lack the ability to enjoy and connect with people who are different from you and your family.

You are unaware of the universes within you and within others, so you believe your ability to welcome others into your neighborhood is limited to the most surface-level aspects of them like their skin color, their accent, the way they dress, or their religious beliefs. It's all you understand about yourself, so it's all you value in others.

This is a symptom of a shallow, uninteresting life. Your mind is boring and superficial, because you set up all these walls around it to stop it from growing. Your heart is hardened and cloistered, because you set up barriers to keep people out. Your spirit is stagnant and impoverished, because you placed too many limitations on its natural outpouring. You're still splashing around in the kiddie pool of the human condition.

It's a waste of a human lifetime to live like this. Open yourself up. Soften your heart. Broaden your mind. Make connections. Delight in the myriad manifestations with which humanity can show up. There is just as much dazzling beauty in other humans as there is in the natural world, and if you can't see it that's a defect in your own character. If you don't learn to grow beyond those limitations, you cut yourself off from unfathomable depths of the human experience that you could instead be taking great joy in.

Don't waste your life on racism. Don't waste your life on Islamophobia, homophobia, transphobia, or any of the other crude ways we cut ourselves off from the connectivity and appreciation that we are all capable of. Deepen your roots and grow into a mature human being. •

Alternate Reality Israel, And Other Reader Questions

Freeman asks on Facebook, "I have quite a few friends/ people in my life who somehow are against the occupation and genocide while also being for Israel. How would you tactfully explain to them why this is a problem?"

The most culturally consequential fictional fantasy land ever authored is not Oz or Narnia or Middle Earth, but the liberal Zionist creation of Alternate Reality Israel.

In the minds of its authors, Alternate Reality Israel exists in a parallel universe at the geographic location of actual real-life Israel, but never became a genocidal apartheid state. In this fictional timeline, Alternate Reality Israel magically came into existence without the mass murder, ethnic cleansing and land theft which would normally be required for the creation of a brand-new ethnostate dropped on top of a pre-existing civilization. Because of magic, Alternate Reality Israel has not needed to use nonstop violence and tyranny to maintain its existence as a theocratic ethnostate, and has instead been able to exist in peace and harmony with all the populations who were living in the area prior to its creation. The position of the liberal Zionist is therefore not self-contradictory, because the existence of Alternate Reality Israel is not at all incompatible with progressive values.

The problem, of course, is that Alternate Reality Israel does not exist, and has never existed. There is no alternate version of Israel that anyone can point to which does not include genocide, apartheid and abuse. The Zionist experiment has been run, and what we see before us is the one and only result of that experiment. This is it. There are no other timelines to compare and contrast this existing reality with.

So when someone says they are "for Israel" but against Israel's occupation and genocide, maybe ask them which "Israel" they are referring to. It can't possibly be the one that exists in this universe, because they said they oppose occupation and genocide. So where is it? Do they have some sort of magical crystal ball which enables them to peer into an alternate universe where Israel somehow isn't doing these things? Show me this kindly, beneficent version of Israel, please.

There isn't any. There never has been. It turns out it was always impossible to create a new state where people were already living and say that a new group of people gets to show up by the millions and run things there, without it looking like nonstop mass-scale abuse. There was never any magical way for that to happen in a way that aligns with human rights and liberal values. Israel was always headed toward this, and everything we're witnessing is the result of what Israel has always been.

If liberals could point to any other Israel (or indeed any other brand new ethnostate placed overtop of a preexisting civilization of a differing ethnicity) which has existed without tremendous injustice, tyranny and abusiveness, then it would be reasonable to say that you support that thing that you are pointing to but not the thing that Israel is now. If they could go "Well with a bit of tweaking Israel could be like the thriving east Asian ethnostate of Zim-Zam" or whatever, then maybe that could be a position with some standing. But no such place exists. All they can say is that they don't support the way Israel actually is in real life. Once they see that, they're seeing clearly.

•

Timothy on YouTube asks, "Why do you not support Zelensky?"

Anyone who still supports Ukrainian president Volodymyr Zelensky is against Ukraine, because Zelensky is acting directly against the will of the overwhelming majority of Ukrainians. Ukrainian men are being violently assaulted and dragged off to fight in a war that a supermajority of Ukrainians now oppose. A recent Gallup poll found that 69 percent of Ukrainians now want a negotiated end to the fighting as soon as possible, with only 24 percent wanting to push on to victory.

But I also opposed the proxy war from the very beginning, because it was a completely unnecessary waste of human life which risked nuclear armageddon and could have been easily avoided with a little diplomacy. It is an extensively documented fact that this war was actively provoked by NATO powers, which was why so many western experts and analysts spent years warning ahead of time that the west's actions were going to lead to war in Ukraine.

No other major power would have allowed a rival power to amass a credible military threat on its border the way NATO was doing to Russia in Ukraine; the last time anyone tried to place a military threat near the United States, Washington responded so aggressively that the world almost ended. It's an unforgivable nightmare that should never have happened, and Zelensky's cronyism toward the US empire helped make it happen.

•

Isaiah on Substack asks, "When you're not actively fighting evil or doing inner work to recover, what do you do for fun?"

Not much, honestly. Tim and I will spend time hanging out with family, we'll sometimes watch a movie or a show to unwind, and I'll play games on my phone here and there, but this is pretty much a 24/7 vocation for us. We don't really have a social life, and fun doesn't feature much. We're generally either working, talking about working, doing inner work, or just loving each other.

We get our enjoyment of life from appreciating beauty everywhere we see it, and from loving, and from our work. To keep things fresh we'll just change up what "work" looks like — that's what the poems and paintings and other art stuff is about. We laugh and joke around a lot, but looking at the way we live our life you'd probably say that we're very serious people.

•

Snow Himbo asks on Twitter, "Given how horrifying reality is at present, what are some things you still have hope in?"

I still have hope in young people. Gen Z haven't just been outperforming all of us on Gaza, they've been leading the charge. They're simply a superior generation to the rest of us. This may be because they didn't grown up marinating in the brainwashing of the mainstream media. It may also be because they're the first generation in human history ever to have the ability to create their own culture without having culture imposed upon them by older generations; they're learning about the world from streamers their own age discussing ideas while playing video games and TikTok personalities explaining politics while putting on makeup. The rest of us got our culture solely from our parents, teachers, Hollywood, and mass media propaganda. We were way more dumbed down, because knowledge was gate-kept from us.

I have hope in the expansion of consciousness. We're growing so much more aware in so many ways, even as things apparently get darker and darker. Gaza is opening eyes at an unprecedented rate. We're growing more and more acutely aware that all the people around the world are human beings with hopes and dreams and feelings and families just like us, even the people who our government and our nation exploit and abuse. People understand the concept of psychological trauma and healing exponentially better than

they did just a few short years ago. We're growing less racist and more accepting of differences, despite the most frenetic efforts of the worst among us.

I still have hope in the collaborative power of the internet. They've tried and tried to shut that down and manipulate it, but we're still finding ways to network and share information at a wildly unprecedented rate, and this has dramatically altered our minds and hearts in some very interesting ways. Because of widespread internet access humanity has arguably changed more in the last twenty years than in the previous twenty thousand, even though we might look and talk more or less the same as we did in the nineties.

I still have hope in activism, because it's working.

I have renewed hope in artists. We're seeing more and more art being made about real things all of a sudden now that they're starting to see how exciting and inspiring it can be to fight back against the war machine.

I still have hope in spiritual awakening. Humanity has a latent potential for radical internal transformation which we haven't really tapped into yet, and it's entirely possible for this potential to emerge as our existential crises push us into the adapt-or-perish moment for our species. If realized at mass scale this could turn things around on a dime.

I still have hope in miracles. I have witnessed far too many in my own life to rule out the possibility of something unexpected coming from way out of left field to knock us off our trajectory toward disaster and dystopia. I know from my own experience that there are dragons lurking within us that are waiting to be uncaged.

I still have hope because of the Palestinians. If they can keep going despite everything they've been through, then we've got a shot too. The other day I saw a guy in Gaza planting a tomato seed in a cut open milk jug, and he was laughing with his friend. They're still finding ways to not only stay alive, but to keep the spark of living alive too. Life finds a way, man. We will find a way. •

"What About My Friends Who Don't Care About Gaza?", And Other Question

Slow Heat asks on Youtube, "Hi Caitlin — question — I have friends, some lifelong, who I don't associate with anymore because, while maybe not supporting, are at the very least ambivalent towards the genocide. I just can't be around people who are more concerned with what show or restaurant they're trying next. Am I the asshole?"

I've been lucky enough not to have anyone significant in my life who doesn't get it, so this isn't an issue that I personally have had to navigate. But I have seen a lot of people struggle with the question of how their interpersonal relationships should be affected by the position that their friends and loved ones take on Gaza.

From where I'm sitting this doesn't look like you're an asshole, it just kind of looks like the natural effects playing out of learning that someone in your life is a shitty person. If you found out that one of your friends likes to torture small animals or drug women and rape them, or that someone in your family watched a child drown in a swimming pool without doing anything, that would naturally change your relationship with them in a permanent way. You would naturally find yourself distancing yourself from them, and things would never be the same.

This wouldn't be your fault, and it also wouldn't be the result of any rule or personal policy that you put in place. People don't normally make a rule for themselves like "never be friends with someone who adores Adolf Hitler," they'd just naturally feel themselves pulling away from anyone who does.

So I don't think this is necessarily something you need to put any amount of thought into, really. This is just what happens when bad people in your life reveal an ugly truth about themselves. If you learn that someone in your life is cool with their government supporting a genocide, you can just sort of let your feelings and natural inclinations lead the way on that.

•

Shiloh on Twitter asks, "Why does no one want to talk about the genocide in Sudan?"

Not that I believe this question is asked in good faith (Shiloh is an Israeli account), but let's answer it anyway.

My government isn't trying to make it illegal for me to criticize the RSF. Every major western institution isn't dedicated to facilitating genocide in Sudan and stomping out all speech which opposes it. My rulers aren't backing a genocide in Sudan and commanding me to support it.

I oppose the genocide that I personally am involved in. When my government and its allies are complicit that makes me complicit,

unless I hold a strong and visible "No." Israel apologists try to frame this as somehow freakish and suspicious when it's obviously the most normal thing in the world.

It's just one of the many, many bad faith ways in which hasbarists try to spin opposing an active genocide as a bad thing. People who ask "Why don't you talk about the bad things those Africans and Asians are doing?" are really just saying "Stop criticizing the white people, criticize the brown people instead. Stop criticizing the worst abuses of the power structure you actually live under and focus on other things."

It's just manipulative concern trolling and genocide apologia.

•

Will on Facebook asks, "Sincerely asking: How do you keep all your posts free? How do you support yourself while keeping your stuff free? I think it's awesome that you do that! But I've found it incredibly difficult to support myself with my writing practice and have been thinking about selling subscriptions so I don't have to take so much other work to survive."

I've written about my funding plan before, but it's been years since I've talked about it, which is weird because it's really one of the most interesting things about this project.

Basically what I've learned is that people really will just support a writer whose work they value without expecting anything in return. It's not a way to get rich, but it pays the rent and puts food on the table just fine.

It's a pure gift economy system. I don't demand anything from my readers, and those who support me don't demand anything of me. I make everything free; I don't do ads, I don't paywall anything, I don't do reward tiers on Patreon, and my free Substack subscription has identical content to the paid one. I just work hard and put everything out there for everyone to read, and invite anyone who feels called to to support what I do. I get to keep working, and they get to know they're helping me do so. And it turns out that's enough.

One thing that helps is that all my platforms and articles contain a notice that anyone who wishes to use or republish my work is free to do so in any way they like free of charge. This has helped grow my audience, because there are always platforms and publications looking for good content to publish. As people get added to my audience across various platforms, a few of them will feel called to help financially support what I do.

It's a model that won't necessarily work for everyone, but it has worked for me, so that's all I can speak to with any authority. If you can only make paid subscriptions or advertising or whatever work for you, then there's absolutely nothing wrong with that either.

•

Kelly on Twitter asks, "Do you think unrelentingly and deeply searching for truth, both inward and outward simultaneously, willing to examine the terrifying things you find, can result in 'enlightenment' regardless of spiritual path, be it Christian, Tao, Jewish, atheist/academic, etc or whatever?"

This is in regard to a previous Q&A in which I discussed the distinction between spirituality and awakening, and the need to expand our awareness of both our own inner processes which give rise to our own individual suffering and of the abusive power dynamics which create so much suffering for humanity collectively.

I think courageously and deeply searching for truth absolutely can lead to enlightenment, so long as your investigation focuses on the nonconceptual aspects of your experience instead of searching for answers in mental stories. Rigorously peering into the nature of self, thought and perception can lead to a dramatic shift in consciousness after which nothing is ever seen the same way again, but trying to figure out your true nature by forming some kind of mental narrative about it will never work.

Awakening is definitely possible regardless of what your religion or non-religion happens to be when you start out, but no religion will ever take you there. That saying "All paths lead to the top of the mountain" or whatever is just nonsense; most paths lead far away from the mountain, or at best just circle the foothills. Religions have very little to do with enlightenment, even the ones that talk about it a lot like Buddhism and Hinduism. Clarity won't come until you discard all belief systems and all your assumptions about what's real and how things work, and start looking at what's actually going on at the most fundamental levels of your own experience.

"It's Not A Genocide" Is Not A Defensible Claim In The Year 2025

•Notes From The Edge Of The Narrative Matrix•

The International Association of Genocide Scholars (IAGS) has determined that Israel is committing genocide in Gaza. This is the world's largest association of genocide scholars, with around 500 experts on the subject including many Holocaust scholars. The consensus was reached by an overwhelming supermajority of the experts — 86 percent, to be exact.

Everyone needs to understand that "there is no genocide in Gaza" is not a claim that can be taken seriously in the year 2025. Amnesty International, Human Rights Watch, UN human rights experts, Israeli human rights groups like B'Tselem, and the overwhelming majority of genocide scholars all agree it's a genocide. The debate is over. The hasbarists lost.

Israel's Foreign Ministry is of course claiming that the IAGS assessment is "entirely based on Hamas's campaign of lies." That's right folks, the genocide scholars are Hamas.

They're just so unbelievably evil. Nobody who's not a cartoon or CGI supervillain has any business being this evil. If you're going to be this insanely evil you should be animated and cackling while twisting your curly mustache all the time.

Possibly the single dumbest thing we are asked to believe about Palestine is that every major human rights institution on earth is part of a secret antisemitic blood libel conspiracy. This genocide is one nonstop insult to our intelligence.

•

Israel is reportedly planning to cut off the small amount of aid it has been allowing in to northern Gaza. This comes after both UN-backed and US-funded hunger monitor groups determined that Israel is causing a famine in Gaza, which was preceded by weeks of Israel furiously denying that it was starving Gaza, which was preceded by Israeli officials openly announcing that they intended to starve Gaza.

•

The western press have been dutifully parroting the US and Israeli government line that Trump's plan for the ethnic cleansing of Gaza will be "voluntary" in their headlines.

"Gaza postwar plan envisions 'voluntary' relocation of entire population," reads a headline from The Washington Post.

"U.S.-run 'Gaza Riviera': Post-war redevelopment plan sees 'voluntary relocation' of millions," says CNBC.

"Trump's Gaza plan involves 'voluntary' relocation of Palestinians — and giving them $5,000 each," says The Independent.

"Gaza post-war plan proposes 'voluntary' relocation, 'tokens' in exchange for land," says France 24.

We're going to be hearing this "voluntary" relocation slogan a lot going forward, and everyone should understand that it's a lie. There is nothing "voluntary" about leaving an area that is being deliberately made uninhabitable by someone with power over you. It's exactly the same as forcing people out at gunpoint.

It is propaganda and journalistic malpractice for the western media to be pushing this slogan.

•

I saw a tweet from liberal influencer Steven Bonnell AKA Destiny saying "Palestine is just fashion for leftists."

Bidenists say this all the time, and it reveals so much about their worldview. They cannot fathom the concept of someone opposing a genocide because genocide is bad; it can only be some kind of trendy fashion statement because it happens to be what's popular right now.

These are people who are not motivated by morality, facts and logic, but solely by selfish and cynical impulses which they then project onto everyone else. They can't imagine anyone doing something because it's the right thing to do, so they have to make up some reason why there must be something in it for them in order for their actions to make sense.

But it is good that even through their own narcissistic, egocentric lens they are beginning to understand that supporting an active genocide has widely become viewed as unacceptable, and that abandoning that insane position is the only way to gain acceptance in mainstream society. Those who can't be brought into line through appeal to compassion and reason can be brought into line through peer pressure and social stigma.

•

When you see the way pro-genocide Jews attack vocally anti-genocide Jews, you understand why there aren't more vocally anti-genocide Jews. This isn't to excuse anyone from their moral obligation to oppose an active genocide, only to point out one of the control mechanisms.

I've watched Zionists constantly try to convince Israeli American academic Shaiel Ben-Ephraim to start drinking again after he switched from defending the genocide to opposing it (he's open about being a recovering alcoholic). I catch flak from Israel supporters 24/7, but I've never had to deal with that level of vitriolic, high-octane hatred. Non-Jews like myself who oppose the Gaza holocaust just don't have to deal with that degree of venom. And that's just what's visible to me online.

Again, this doesn't excuse the moral obligation that Jews and non-Jews alike have to oppose Israel's genocidal atrocities. I'm just pointing out one of the many abusive dynamics used to maintain the status quo. •

If Israel Stops Fighting, A Genocide Ends; If Hamas Stops Fighting, Ethnic Cleansing Moves Forward

•Notes From The Edge Of The Narrative Matrix•

You always see Israel apologists saying "If Hamas lays down its arms there'll be no more war, if Israel lays down its arms there'll be no more Israel."

But really the exact opposite is true. If the Israelis lay down their arms, a genocide ends. If Hamas lays down their arms, Israel's planned ethnic cleansing of Gaza happens quickly and without resistance.

Israel has been very clear and explicit about the fact that its onslaught in Gaza will not end until Trump's plan for the ethnic cleansing of the Gaza Strip is completed. Hamas could surrender and release all the hostages today and this ethnic cleansing agenda would still move forward as planned, according to Israel's top officials. They've been completely unambiguous about this.

Anyone who says this nightmare would end if Hamas surrenders is lying. All that would happen if Hamas surrenders is Palestinians being purged from a Palestinian territory forever.

•

Israeli politicians and official government social media accounts have begun pushing the narrative that Muslim immigrants are a threat to Europe, the implication being that Europeans should support Israel because Israel is helping to kill the Muslims.

Israel's Arabic language Twitter account recently posted a graph showing the number of Mosques across Europe accompanied by right wing "great replacement"-style talking points, saying that "This is the true face of colonization. And this is what is happening while Europe is oblivious and does not care about the danger."

Former Israeli prime minister Naftali Bennett tweeted last month that "Europe is becoming Islamized," fearmongering about the number of Muslim immigrants throughout Europe.

Benjamin Netanyahu tweeted on Wednesday that "Belgian Prime Minister de Wever is a weak leader who seeks to appease Islamic terrorism by sacrificing Israel. He wants to feed the terrorist crocodile before it devours Belgium."

They don't want Muslims to live in Palestine. They don't want Muslims to live in Europe. Kinda seems like they just don't want Muslims to live.

•

Haaretz reports that an IDF commander named Haim Cohen received intelligence warnings immediately prior to the Hamas attack on the Nova music festival on October 7 but took no preemptive action, and that "Cohen was also the officer who initially approved the festival on Tuesday of that week."

This is just the latest addition to a large body of evidence that Israel appears to have intentionally allowed the October 7 attack to happen after deliberately provoking it in order to advance a preexisting agenda to steal more Palestinian territory.

•

President Trump is reportedly preparing to change the name of the Department of Defense back to the Department of War, which was what the US military department was called until shortly after WWII.

I'm seeing some criticism of this move, but personally I think it's fine. When was the last time the US used its military for defensive purposes? Calling it the War Department is just calling it what it is. Might as well be honest about it.

•

Defense Secretary Pete Hegseth (soon to be Secretary of War, I guess) announced that we can expect to see more strikes on Venezuelan ships after a deadly US attack on a boat which the Trump administration claims was trafficking drugs.

"We have assets in the air, assets in the water, assets on ships because this is a deadly serious mission for us, and it won't stop … with just this strike," Hegseth told the press on Wednesday.

Secretary of State Marco Rubio said "I don't care what the UN says" when challenged by the press about his assertions regarding Venezuela's responsibility for America's drug problems, claiming that "Maduro is an indicted drug trafficker in the United States and he's a fugitive of American justice."

You really couldn't get a more honest representation of US foreign policy than the top American diplomat saying "I don't care what the UN says" and then claiming that the leaders of sovereign nations are subject to "American justice". These freaks really do believe this entire planet is their property.

As we discussed previously, this is just cover for a longstanding regime change agenda against an oil-rich socialist government that Washington has sought to depose for many years. Venezuela's role in the drug trade is severely overstated and its role in the Fentanyl epidemic is nonexistent. This is about oil, capitalism, and geostrategic control.

•

Fame is so weird in our society. People spend all this effort becoming great at something, they get a bunch of fans, then they get thrown into this strange, cloistered universe of immense wealth and social circles full of psychopaths and parasitic middle men and highly neurotic individuals, and they go nuts and lose what it is that their fans fell in love with in the first place. Happens over and over again.

Under capitalism success as an artist means losing your art. •

https://www.caitlinjohnst.one

www.ingramcontent.com/pod-product-compliance
Lightning Source LLC
Chambersburg PA
CBHW081202270326
41930CB00014B/3262